Read this book cover to cover... and lov keeping it real, telling it how it is, with down to earth tips on leadership, communicating with impact and building and keeping trust. It starts with being true to yourself—and sharing, showing and keeping it real with others. Thanks Gabrielle for the stories, the reminders and the advice! Needed today more than ever."

Christine Corbett, former acting CEO and Chief Customer Officer of Australia Post

Authenticity is a word that gets thrown around a lot. Gabrielle is the first leadership expert I've met who lives it. Real messages, delivered with truth in a way that anyone can access."

Matt Church, Author, Speaker and Founder Thought Leaders

I have often reflected on the many presentations I have sat through and when I have been on the edge of my seat or when I have been trying desperately to stay awake. And what was the difference? Well it was rarely the content but nearly always the way it was delivered. Real Communication is one of those 'must read' books for anyone who is serious about leadership as it is packed with practical tips and real-life examples of how to lead and communicate in a more effective and authentic way."

Jamie McPhee, CEO ME Bank

Real Communication: How to be you and lead true is in equal parts entertaining as it is instructional. It is teeming with tips, tools and lively anecdotes from the battle of Actium to the battle for same sex marriage, highlighting the importance of jargon free communication and authentic self.

In a world of fake media riddled with message obfuscation, Ral, with the wisdom of an expert who has helped leaders become outstanding communicators, tells it like it is and makes simple the art of Real Communication.

I highly recommend Real Communication both for the tools, tips and practical insights it provides as well as for the simple yet profound reminder that if you bring self-awareness and authenticity into each interaction, you end up doing a service not only for yourself but also for those you interact with. Here's to Real Communication and bring on the f-bomb!"

Dorothy Hisgrove, Partner and Chief People Officer PwC

" The irrepressible and talented Gabrielle Dolan has done it again. Real Communication *is full of wonderful stories and useful tips, all in the service of enabling people wherever they sit to be more effective in getting their message heard and absorbed, and in exercising leadership on behalf of whatever they care deeply about.*"

Marty Linsky, Faculty Harvard Kennedy School

" *The field of leadership has evolved a great deal since the turn of the century. People are now wanting to lead in a way that is more authentic and bring their entire selves to work. With pressing concerns for diversity and inclusion,* Real Communication: How to Be You and Lead True *provides essential insights for twenty first century leaders. It's a refreshing – and necessary – view of where leadership is headed.*"

Frederique Covington, Senior Vice President Marketing Asia Pacific, VISA

" *In our fast changing world, our customers and employees' expectations have evolved faster than ever before. Jargon, command and control leadership just doesn't work anymore, especially for the younger generations. People are looking for and will respond to genuine and authentic leadership they can trust.*

This book will make you completely rethink how you lead, communicate and behave to be a more inclusive leader and possibly reassess your own values to be successful in the future, professionally and personally."

Michael Ebeid AM, Group Executive, Enterprise at Telstra

" *Having the courage to be you when communicating takes lots of skill and practice and Gabrielle's insights and simple clear approach allows the reader to go on their own learning journey.*

As someone who genuinely cares for people, it is so important to put your audience at the centre of your communication style, approach and delivery and Gabrielle shows you how to do this in a very transparent and genuine way.

Most organisations talk about the need to grow and innovate and to do this leaders need to create an environment of trust, inclusion and engagement. At the heart of this is the ability to communicate in a simple, compelling and genuine way free of jargon and acronyms and with the right emotion to connect with the people of the organisation to deliver their best every single day. Gabrielle's book is your own co-pilot, as it is full of ideas to support you on your journey."

Kate Mason, Group Director, People & Culture, Coca-Cola Amatil

REAL
COMMUNICATION

GABRIELLE DOLAN
REAL
COMMUNICATION
HOW TO BE YOU AND LEAD TRUE

WILEY

First published in 2019 by John Wiley & Sons Australia, Ltd
42 McDougall St, Milton Qld 4064

Office also in Melbourne

Typeset in ITC Berkeley Oldstyle Std 11/14pt

© John Wiley & Sons Australia, Ltd 2019

The moral rights of the author have been asserted

A catalogue record for this book is available from the National Library of Australia

Cover design by Wiley

Author photo by Oli Sansom

10 9 8 7 6 5 4 3 2 1

CONTENTS

THE REAL RAL

I am one of eight children. My littlest sister could never pronounce 'Gabrielle', so she called me 'Ral' instead and the name has since stuck.

It was probably being one of so many that first helped me realise the power of storytelling. It was a great way to gain some attention from my parents.

During my 20s, storytelling's power was reinforced while sitting in pubs with my mates. We would spend the night sharing stories, fuelled by alcohol and '80s music — which was (and still is) a magical combination.

This obsession with storytelling (not '80s music... okay, maybe a little) continued into adult life and my career in a senior leadership role at National Australia Bank. It was here that I realised stories could be used for good, and for business — and, more importantly, for the good of the business!

Since that time, I have made it my mission to teach others how to share stories in business to communicate more effectively and authentically. I've worked with thousands of high-profile leaders and companies from around the world to help them get real with their communications. These companies have included Amazon, Shell, Caltex, Ericsson, Accenture, EY, VISA, Uber and International Committee Red Cross (to name-drop a few).

I might have failed my final year of English, but I didn't let that hold me back. This is my fifth book and my old English teacher Mrs Bennetts would be proud and no doubt extremely surprised of this effort. My other books include *Stories for Work: The Essential Guide to Business Storytelling* (Wiley, 2017), *Ignite: Real Leadership, Real Talk, Real Results* (Wiley, 2015) *Storytelling for Job Interviews* (self-published, 2016), and *Hooked: How Leaders Connect, Engage and Inspire with Storytelling* (Wiley, 2013).

I hold a master's degree in management and leadership from Swinburne University, and an associate diploma in education and training from the University of Melbourne. I'm also a graduate of the Harvard Kennedy School of Executive Education in both the Art and Practice of Leadership Development, and Women and Power: Leadership in a New World—and I have the T-Shirt and coffee mug to prove it.

My obsession for bringing authenticity to the way business people communicate led me to found Jargon Free Fridays in 2016 (www. jargonfreefridays.com). This is a fun way to raise awareness about the consequence of jargon and acronyms.

I live in Melbourne with my husband, Steve, two teenage daughters, Alex and Jess, and Digger the dog—though often I'm found in the veggie patch on my holiday property at Bermagui in New South Wales.

I think (no, I know) the world would be a better place if there was more manure in vegetable gardens and less in business. Don't you agree?

Ral

REALLY BIG THANKS

For some reason this book felt like the hardest book I have ever written... maybe it's just the recency of pain. Like when you finish a long run or give birth. But I am so proud of the end result of this book and I would not have been able to achieve this without the help from the following people.

Firstly, the always brilliant (and sometimes brutal) Kelly Irving who is an amazing editor. This is the third book Kelly has edited for me and her feedback and suggestions are always insightful. Like a personal trainer, her tough love and guidance always takes my writing to a higher level.

I would also like to thank the team at Wiley for their ongoing support in me. Special shout out to Lucy Raymond, Ingrid Bond and Charlotte Duff for their guidance and suggestions. It's always a pleasure to work with them.

Massive gratitude to Kieran Flanagan who was the inspiration for the cover design and for Matt Church, Janine Garner and Dan Gregory who gave me the courage to go with a photo of me on the cover. I seriously had to get out of my own way there.

Speaking of which, Oli Sansom is a magical photographer who is not only a pleasure to work with but beautifully captured the look and feel I was after. He made me scrub up OK.

Another really big thanks to my Executive Manager and friend Elise Turner who basically kept the show running while I buried myself away writing for days and weeks on end. Every time I went looking for a distraction, which was fairly often, she reverted to her school teacher days and I was told to keep writing.

Special thanks to my family, Steve, Alex and Jess who give me not only the space to write but often some pretty good material to write about. And if I don't mention Digger the dog I get in trouble, so thanks to Digger for keeping me company in the office, even though he seriously stunk at times.

This book would not be possible without all the people that kindly gave me their time and stories to feature in this book...and quite a few others I interviewed that due to a change of direction in some parts, didn't end up in the book. I thank you for allowing me to share your stories, insights and opinions.

Finally, thanks to you, the reader. It is only through people like you that have the courage to be you and lead true that we will have genuine and real communication.

INTRODUCTION

This is just what the world needs, isn't it? Another bloody book on communication and leadership.

Well, I might not be the best salesperson in the world, but let me explain why I wrote this book and why you need to read it.

I have worked in business for over 35 years (which does make me feel a tad old …). For a big chunk of that time, I have helped leaders communicate more effectively and be the absolute best that they can be: authentic, insightful, impactful, influential … just plain real.

I know from personal experience how hard it is to work for, and work with, leaders who talk rubbish and never do what they say they do. (I don't think I am on my own here.) We are crying out for leaders who are authentic and speak in a way that is real.

This kind of authentic leadership and real communication
is needed now, more than ever.

Why? Times have changed, and continue to change at a rapid rate (it's not slowing down!). With this change comes a whole new set of phrases, acronyms and jargon that is confusing and, at times, overwhelming. We are also more cynical of the world at large and, hence, more demanding of what we expect from the companies and leaders we work for.

So in part I of this book, we will explore the decline of trust in today's world and our confusion about knowing what or whom to trust. We'll also look at the evolving expectations of employees and customers, and why they are crying out for us to communicate to them in a more transparent and genuine way. And we'll examine the increasing amount of corporate jargon that we use and how that can be disengaging and isolating. Finally, we will look at our addiction to acronyms and how that can lead to inefficient communication and, in many cases, miscommunication.

In part II, you'll discover some practical ways to ensure you communicate concisely by putting your audience first. We will look at the need to include emotion and stories in your communication if you want to form a genuine connection with employees and customers. You'll also learn how to prepare your content so it's more engaging and visual, helping you deliver messages with impact — no matter if you're writing an email, talking one-to-one, holding a team meeting, pitching to a client or speaking on stage to a large audience.

Then in part III, we'll dive into what it really means to be an authentic leader. Through case studies and stories, you will experience what it looks like to have the clarity to use real words, and the courage to deal with what is real and admit when you have stuffed up. We will look in depth at leaders who have congruence in their values and actions, and who show what is real to them and the people they lead.

Throughout the book I've included real-life examples, stories and case studies from my clients as well as high-profile companies. And at the end of all chapters in parts II and III, I've included 'Get REAL now' pointers and tips to help you apply the information provided to your communication and leadership. These examples and pointers will help you to see what real leadership looks like in practice and, ultimately, how you can get real with your employees, customers and colleagues.

We are all crying out for real communication and authentic leadership.

This book will show you why and how.

PART I

Why you need to get REAL now

It is more important than ever that we communicate in a way that is genuine, authentic and real. This is because of four worldwide trends that are influencing how effective we are when we communicate to others.

The four trends are:

- *Decline in trust:* We're surrounded by alternative facts, fake news and cover-ups. Royal commissions and inquiries have revealed years of systematic deceit, lies and betrayals of trust. It's no surprise that we are sceptical. Leaders need to be mindful of this cynicism when they are communicating to employees, customers and peers, especially in times of change.

- *Evolution of expectations:* Over the past decade, our expectations of how we work, how we lead and how we are communicated to has changed. The challenge is how we respond to this. Leaders need a new mindset and new skills to communicate and lead differently, while companies need updated processes and structures that encourage everyone to get and feel involved, regardless of their age or background.

- *Rise of jargon:* We use jargon as a default in business to help us fit in, to make us sound smarter than we are or to avoid saying what we really mean. The overall result? Miscommunication and the feeling of isolation as we struggle to understand what is being said by the people we work for, the companies we buy from, the peers we work with and even the kids we parent.

- *Addiction to acronyms:* Every acronym has a multiple meaning or interpretation. So if everyone has the same understanding and is clear on what a particular acronym stands for and means, great! However, if they are not (and the vast majority of the time they are not), using the acronym can lead to inefficiency, miscommunication and, in some cases, very embarrassing situations.

We'll explore each of these trends in detail in part I.

CHAPTER 1

DECLINE IN TRUST

Here's how the Oxford Dictionary defines trust:

1. Firm belief in the reliability, truth, or ability of someone or something.

2. Acceptance of the truth of a statement without evidence or investigation.

3. The state of being responsible for someone or something.

4. A person or duty for which one has responsibility.

And here's how trust works in practice. I give my house key to my cleaners because I trust them to come in and clean my home when I'm not there and not damage or steal anything. My parents have a key to my place as a legacy from when they used to babysit the kids. My friend has a key in case I lock myself out and I can't get in, so too does my executive manager for when she needs to come to my house and work.

Trust makes our life, at home and work, easier.

If I didn't have trust, I would have to stay home every time the cleaners come.

The Cambridge Dictionary has a slightly different definition for trust from the Oxford, defining it as, 'To believe that someone is good and honest and will not harm you, or something is safe and reliable'. I think this aspect is so true when you look not just at the people around you—your friends, your leaders, your team, your peers and your clients—but also at the information you are presented with by those people.

We trust financial institutions with our money and superannuation. We trust our accountants to ensure they file our tax legally. We trust our insurance companies to pay out if we get sick or our house burn downs. We trust our local barista when they say they serve organic coffee and won't make it too hot. We trust our kids when they say they don't have any homework.[1]

The flip side to all of this is that when we lose trust, life becomes much, much harder.

Without trust, we don't make decisions as quickly or we take more time to double check information. If we don't trust our doctor, we seek out a second or perhaps third opinion. If we don't trust our accountant, we spend a large amount of time checking and double-checking the tax statements. If we don't trust our partners, we spend a lot of time thinking and expecting the worst.

As a leader, if your people don't trust you, they will not follow you. And if you look over your shoulder and no-one is following you, guess what? You may have the title of leader but you are not a leader. The title is all you have.

If you are a business and customers lose trust in you, you lose their loyalty and their spending dollars. And when it comes out that an abuse of trust has been performed deliberately, this can cause enormous brand damage—which, you will soon see, is near impossible to repair. Once lost, trust is very hard to earn back.

Knowing who to trust and what to trust has become significantly harder.

---

[1] Well, maybe we are a little bit suspicious of that.

Who do you trust?

Edelman, a global communications marketing firm, conduct an annual global study to determine levels of trust. The 2018 results revealed that we are in a battle for the truth, and knowing who we can trust to provide this. The research showed an overall decline in trust, specifically in the United States, where they experienced the steepest decrease for any country (out of the 28 included in the research) ever measured over the 18 years of this study.

The report also looked at the levels of trust in four institutions:

1. media

2. government

3. business

4. non-government organisations.

Findings from the report showed:

- Non-government organisations are distrusted in 10 countries and have seen a decline in trust in 14 of the 28 included countries over the past year from 2017 to 2018.

- While business has experienced an increase in trust in 14 out of the 28 countries, it is still distrusted overall in 18 countries.

- Trust in government has also increased, this time in 16 countries, but they are still distrusted in 21 of the 28 countries.

One of the perhaps most disturbing findings is that for the first time media is the most distrusted institution, being distrusted in 22 of the 28 countries. The study classifies media as both content (what is being communicated) and platform (how it is being communicated, including traditional TV and radio but also social media platforms such as Facebook). While trust in *journalists* rose 5 points to 59, trust in *platforms* dropped 2 points to 51.

Overall, 59 per cent of participants stated that they were not sure what is true and what is not, 56 per cent stated that they do not know which politicians to trust and 42 per cent say they do not know which companies or brands to trust.

This lack of trust in the media—both in content and platform—has largely arisen due to the rise of fake news and alternative facts.

The birth of 'alternative facts'

When did alternative facts replace lies? Well, after Donald Trump's US presidential inauguration in 2017, Sean Spicer, his press secretary at the time, stated that present at the event was 'the largest audience to ever witness an inauguration. Period'.

The backlash was swift, with images popping up over media comparing Barack Obama's inauguration crowd side by side with Trump's. The fact was that the images showed the crowd on the streets of Washington DC for Obama were far larger than the number who turned up for Trump. Period.

After making that statement, Spicer told the media that he would be honest with the American people, but also stated that the White House may sometimes 'disagree with facts'.

That same day, the US Counselor to the President, Kellyanne Conway, was interviewed on *Meet the Press* and was asked to defend the White House and Sean Spicer's false statement about the attendance numbers at Trump's inauguration. When challenged on why Spicer would 'utter a provable falsehood', Conway replied that Spicer was giving 'alternative facts'.

Conway's choice of words was widely mocked on social media and criticised by journalists. It was described as a 'George Orwell phrase' and even helped increase sales of his book, *1984*, pushing it to the number one bestseller position on Amazon and forcing a 75 000 reprint by publisher Penguin.

Conway later defended the phrase, defining 'alternative facts' as 'additional facts and alternative information'.

Surely alternative facts would be more accurately defined as lies.

If we have the highest office in the United States claiming alternative facts as real, that this is having a negative impact on trust overall is hardly a surprise.

Faking it

'Fake news' is another term that has entered our modern-day vocabulary.

Of course, fake news is nothing new. Cases have been recorded as far back as the first century BC, when Octavian apparently ran a fake news campaign against his rival Mark Antony, publishing a false document of Mark Antony's will, which stated that he wished to be entombed in the mausoleum of the Ptolemaic pharaohs. This invoked outrage from the Roman people, who were already unhappy with Mark Antony marrying[2] Cleopatra (after divorcing Octavian's sister) and appointing her ruler of Egypt, Cyprus, Crete and Syria.

After Mark Antony was defeated by Octavian at the Battle of Actium, Cleopatra was forced to flee to Egypt so she spread fake news of her own suicide. However, she forgot to tell her husband (a major oversight, which some historians argue was deliberate) and he thought she was really dead, so he committed suicide himself.

Fake news is the deliberate spreading of fabricated information with the intention to deceive, typically for political or financial gain.

This kind of deception seems to be on the rise as advances in technology make fake news more believable. For example, researchers have developed programs that allow you to swap faces on videos. With an application such as FakeApp (which started life as a program enabling users to make fake celebrity porn), people can create very convincing fake videos about anything they choose. The capability—and accessibility—of this technology means it is very easy for anyone with a bit of technical know-how to create fake news.

This technology is not only making fake news more convincing and, therefore, easier to believe, but is also allowing it to be spread at a faster rate and to reach more people. While news in the past was communicated by traditional print and mainstream media outlets, it is now increasingly being spread by social media.

New technologies for creating fake audio are also on the market. Programs allow you to edit audio in much the same way as you can edit

[2] There's even dispute around if they ever actually were married.

a photo. The Canadian company Lyrebird, for example, allows you to fake someone else's voice.

So emerging technologies will literally allow you to create an audio clip of anyone saying anything. This could have some serious repercussions, with people being forced to defend an audio clip of something they never actually said or, conversely, people easily being able to deny something they did say, claiming it as fake audio. Imagine the impact that could have on political campaigns!

Some people may create fake news to undermine their opponents or to elevate themselves. Some even do it for fun or satire.

In any case, this has a significant impact on who and what we trust.

The Edelman report mentioned earlier in this chapter stated that 7 out of 10 participants were worried that false information in fake news will be used as a weapon. The report also showed that 63 per cent agreed the average person does not know how to tell good journalism from rumours of falsehoods, and that 59 per cent agreed it is becoming harder to tell if a piece of news was produced by a respected media institution.

With an increase in citizen journalism, where anyone looking for 15 minutes of fame with a smartphone can provide newsworthy content to mainstream media channels, plus more convincing technology readily available to us, distrust looks set to increase.

Trust me, it's important

As can be seen from the focus areas in the Edelman report, in society we delegate important aspects of our lives to four major institutions:

1. media, for information and knowledge

2. government, to provide national security and public policy

3. business, for our economic and wellbeing needs

4. non-government organisations, for social causes and issues.

Edelman believe that in order for us to feel safe with this delegation, 'we need to trust them to act with integrity and with our best interest in mind'. But when we don't believe these institutions are acting in this way, distrust starts to set in.

They also suggest that 'trust is a forward looking metric' and is an indicator of whether people will find you credible in the future. As opposed to reputation, which is based on previous behaviour.

Trust is a critical asset that institutions, companies and individuals need to fight for.

Let's look at the finance industry as a case in point on why trust is so important. According to Edelman's 2018 report, the finance industry was the least trusted industry of all. This finding is backed up by Deloitte, who in July 2018 released their recent research into the Australian financial industry, where they'd surveyed over 1000 Australian consumers. The insights in this report show that trust in the Australian financial services industry had 'taken a dive'. The report stated that:

- 32 per cent of customers said their trust in the finance industry had deteriorated in the previous 12 months

- 25 per cent of customers did not trust the financial services industry, with banking and insurance the least trusted

- 47 per cent (that's almost half) of customers did not trust their own financial service provider.

To really show the extent of distrust in the financial services industry in Australia, 23 per cent of those surveyed said they would consider switching to financial services provided by an airline carrier such as Qantas and Virgin.

This insight, I believe, shows not only how far the finance industry has fallen in the eyes of its customers but also how important trust is.

We have lost so much faith in the traditional finance industry that we are considering having our financial services needs met by airline carriers. When we lose trust in companies or industries, we will naturally seek what they offer elsewhere, even if what we seek is not that organisation's main area of expertise! I trust Qantas with my life every time I fly with them, so is it really too much of a stretch to trust them with my superannuation or savings?

This is a real danger for traditional finance companies as new players enter the market and provide more choice for customers. As Sean Pillot de Chenecey says in his 2018 book *The Post-Truth Business*, 'If a brand isn't trustworthy, when choice is available it'll be rejected in favour of one that is'.

Companies need to be more aware that, along with losing business to their competitors due to a lack of trust, they can also lose business to other industries.

From 2013 to 2018, Australia went through two royal commissions into institutions that just a generation ago were the pinnacle of trust in society. The Royal Commission into Institutional Responses to Child Sexual Abuse investigated many religious institutions, mainly the Catholic Church, and the Royal Commission into Misconduct in the Banking, Superannuation and Financial Services Industry investigated finance institutions.

The Royal Commission into Misconduct in the Banking, Superannuation and Financial Services Industry uncovered:

- systematic processes for forging documents

- failing to verify customers' living expenses before lending them money

- selling insurance to people who couldn't afford it

- selling insurance to people who could never claim on it

- charging fees to people who had died

- charging fees for no service

- lying to regulators.

To the big question of why these failures happened, the interim report stated 'Too often, the answer seems to be greed—the pursuit of short-term profit at the expense of basic standards of honesty'. These findings have created significant trust issues for the organisations involved.

Trust comes with a high price.

What does losing trust cost?

In 2015, the German car manufacturer Volkswagen admitted cheating on emissions tests in the United States. Named the 'diesel dupe', the US Environmental Protection Agency found that many Volkswagen diesel cars had software called a 'defeat device' installed in their engines. This software was specifically installed in cars to allow them to cheat the US emissions tests, with the installation then being systematically covered up.

The year prior to the cheating being discovered, US regulators had raised concerns with Volkswagen about their emissions levels, but the company claimed the levels were the result of 'technical issues' and originally denied any claims of discrepancy.

The eventual discovery of the cheating led to millions of cars worldwide being recalled, at an estimated cost of $US18 billion. Volkswagen's share price fell by one-third days after the scandal broke.

In the wake of the scandal, Volkswagen US CEO Michael Horn said, 'We've totally screwed up'. The Volkswagen parent group's chief executive at the time, Martin Winterkorn, said his company had 'broken the trust of our customers and the public'. Winterkorn resigned as a direct result of the scandal and was replaced by Matthias Mueller, the former head of Porsche. One of Mueller's first statements was, 'My most urgent task is to win back trust for the Volkswagen Group'.

In January 2017, Volkswagen pleaded guilty to criminal charges and admitted that their engineers had developed the defeat devices because their diesel models could not pass the US emissions standards without them. They were fined US$2.8 billion.

Former CEO Winterkorn was charged with fraud and conspiracy in May 2018.

Cheating isn't cheap, and it could have long-term, serious repercussions. So you've got to ask yourself, is it really worth it?

Why it's so hard to rebuild trust

In Australia in September 2018, most of the larger banks raised their interest rates—except for NAB, with group Chief Executive Officer (at the time) Andrew Thorburn stating the need to rebuild trust as the contributing factor behind their decision. In a video to the market, Thorburn said, 'We need to rebuild the trust of our customers...By focusing more on our customers, we build trust and advocacy, and this creates a more sustainable business'.

Analysts estimate that for every month NAB does not raise their rates as the other banks have, they are forgoing approximately $29 million[3]. Some analysts have said this move is a gamble, while some have said it's a great PR stunt. The reality is that NAB, as well as the rest of the finance industry—not to mention many of our religious and political leaders—need to rebuild trust but it has to be genuine.

Attempts to rebuild trust cannot be faked.

Let's look at Facebook as another example. In 2018, Facebook launched a global marketing campaign in a bid to win back their customers' trust after Facebook allowed an app to access users' data without users knowing. They ended up harvesting the profiles of a reported 87 million users around the world during 2014 and 2015. This information was later used by Cambridge Analytica in the 2016 US presidential campaign to influence voters. It was not until 2018—and following the courage of a whistle blower—that this was discovered.

The TV advert Facebook launched to win back trust starts with a voiceover, 'We came here for the friends', and continues with 'But then something happened. We had to deal with spam, click bait, fake news and data misuse. That's going to change. From now on, Facebook will do more to keep you safe and protect your privacy'. The advert ends with 'Because when this place does what it was built for, we all get a little closer'.

Ironically, Facebook's attempt to win back their customers' trust had the opposite effect. Most people took the advert as a blatant attempt to position

---

[3] They did raise interest rates months later on 27 January 2019.

the spam, click bait, fake news and data misuse as something that happened to Facebook, without any acknowledgement of the part Facebook played in contributing to the issues. All we really wanted was an apology.

The problem with severing trust is that when trust is broken, it is extremely hard to restore.

We probably all know this on a personal level from when a colleague, friend, family member or partner has betrayed our trust. The pain from this is the worst kind of emotional pain. When we trust people, we rely on them and when this is broken—and especially when it is broken deliberately—we feel betrayed. Sometimes we even feel naive for putting our trust in the person in the first place, and feel guilty that it's somehow our fault.

Betrayal, guilt and faith...they are some serious emotions. This is why, at the very heart of it, trust is emotional. It's not logical or rational, and that's why rebuilding trust is so hard.

Token 'tick the box' exercises will not cut it when it comes to rebuilding trust. Attempts to rebuild trust need to be authentic. Ralph Waldo Emerson, an American philosopher, famously once wrote, 'What you are stands over you the while, and thunders so that I cannot hear what you say to the contrary'. Put another way, your actions will speak louder than your carefully crafted words.

It is perhaps one of the main reasons why real words, genuine communication and authentic leadership are needed more than ever before.

CHAPTER 2

EVOLUTION OF EXPECTATIONS

I have a pretty close relationship with my two teenage daughters, and they talk to me about anything (well, within reason). Yet, I know the conversations I have with them are very different from the conversations I have had with my parents — both now and when I was growing up.

The way we communicate with our kids, in most cases, has dramatically changed from generation to generation. I mean, who else remembers their mum or dad saying that 'children should be seen and not heard'?

Nowadays, our children, from as young as toddler age, are not only invited to sit at the dining table, but are also expected to be involved in the conversation. They, in turn, expect to contribute and be listened to! This is likely why they also expect a seat around the boardroom table, even if metaphorical. Their expectations are different from ours; their expectations have evolved.

Everyone's expectations have evolved—not only about the type of work we do, but also about the way we are communicated to and the type of leadership we expect.

Now let's look at what happens when these different generations, with their different expectations, meet in the workforce.

We currently have four different generations in the workforce:

1. *Baby boomers:* Born mid-1940s to mid-1960s.

2. *Generation X:* Born mid-1960s to late 1970s.

3. *Generation Y (otherwise known as millennials or gen next):* Born early 1980s to mid-1990s.

4. *Generation Z (also known as post-millennials or iGeneration):* Born mid-1990s to 2010.

(Gen alpha is the newest generation and includes those born after 2010, but those in this grouping are still too young to be entering the workforce.)

Striking the right balance between different generations is becoming a real challenge for companies managing the expectations of their employees.

What do *they* want?

Holly Ransom, CEO of the consultancy Emergent, is considered one of the world's leading authorities on intergenerational leadership and communication. She explains that the younger generation are looking for three aspects when it comes to work:

1. purpose

2. flexibility

3. connection.

I'd say these three areas are now increasingly important to everyone in the workforce, not just the younger generation.

So let's look at what each means in more detail and then consider the consequences and challenges they bring to leadership and communication.

Purpose

I spent my first 12 months in the workforce as a trainee computer operator. This meant I got to do all the boring jobs: restocking paper into printers, fixing printer jams and sorting out where those documents had to be mailed to. I might do this for a week and then the following week would spend my time loading tapes into tape machines or cartridges into cartridge drives. That's just the way it was — back then. But try treating a new employee or graduate like that now and you will lose them before the year is out!

In 2018 the National Society of High School Scholars interviewed over 16 000 college and high-school students (part of gen Z) across the United States. The research uncovered that expectations for their jobs were very high. More than 75 per cent of respondents anticipated going to graduate school and wanted to be working in a related and meaningful field within six months of graduation. Six months!

That means no boring jobs involving tape changing or restocking paper. Members of gen Y, Z, alpha and whatever will come after, are not prepared to go through years of a boring job on the promise of a better one. They want to be doing work they love—and feel like this work has purpose—as soon as they enter the workforce and I seriously don't blame them for that.

We want to feel we are contributing to a higher sense of something and not just profit for the company.

The 2018 Deloitte Millennial Survey showed that millennials and members of generation Z 'yearn for leaders whose decisions might benefit the world and their careers'.

One of the key findings from this survey was that respondents' opinions about the motivations and ethics of companies indicated a sharp decline after trending upwards for the previous two years. The report showed that while millennials realise profits are important, they also believe businesses should consider all stakeholders' interests. The report also states that 'loyalty must be earned' and that most millennials are prepared to leave companies, and leave them quickly, for a better workplace experience.

Individual leaders must determine what is important for the people they lead and how they can help them achieve that purpose.

A real opportunity exists for companies and individual leaders to start meeting the expectations of this generation and become the leaders for positive change through focusing on purpose not just profits.

Flexibility

When I started work, the term 'flexible work' just didn't exist. My first job still had manual punch cards that worked in 15-minute time slots. (Yes, really!) The only flexibility I had was if I punched in within seven minutes of my start time, I was not considered late. If I punched in one minute later, I was docked 15 minutes' pay.

Gradually over the years, and over the course of changing jobs, working from home became the new thing. At first, this was difficult for two reasons:

- *Technology made it clunky* — this was before fast-speed internet connections, and laptops were heavy and bulky.

- *It was seen as a privilege* — working away from supervision was frowned upon by most employers and employees, or deemed something for the 'lucky few'.

Now, of course, wi-fi, compact laptops and the cloud mean you can almost work from anywhere. My office, for example, can be the back of an Uber, an airport lounge, a café or my home office — all in the space of one day.

Our evolving expectations, regardless of generation, mean that this flexibility is no longer a privilege but a given. More and more employees are working flexibly — regardless of their age. I have one client who is in her 50s and works as a senior executive in marketing, and her non-negotiable for any new role she applies for is working from home every Friday.

In addition, more and more organisations are encouraging flexible work arrangements. In 2017, EY (formally Ernst & Young) Australia and New Zealand renamed October as Flextober and encouraged their employees to work flexibly — and post images of their working arrangements on internal and external social media sites. The driver behind this was to encourage people to talk about flexible working and get more senior people role modelling it. The campaign was so successful that in 2018 other regions in the company, including Asia, Europe, Africa, India, the Middle East and the United States, all jumped on board the initiative.

A 2017 global workforce survey conducted by Polycom, titled 'The Changing World of Work', surveyed over 24 000 people in 12 countries. Responses in the survey showed that productivity and teamwork are both significantly improved when employees can choose where they work, with 98 per cent of respondents agreeing that working flexibly boosts productivity.

The survey also revealed that 62 per cent of the global working population is already working flexibly—more than ever before.

Working flexibly is the new norm, which brings benefits as well as new challenges to how we connect and communicate.

Connection

Remember when corporate communication was tightly controlled with a top-down cascading approach, not too dissimilar to a champagne tower? You know the set up—as the champagne filled the top glasses, it would spill over to the next level underneath. Eventually, in the glasses at the bottom of the tower, you'd be lucky if you got a few dregs to enjoy. Very rarely would you end up with a full glass like the levels above you.

Back then, communication involved a certain hierarchy. However, nowadays this slow, cascading approach has shifted to a more connected, faster one.

We want to feel connected and able to talk to our team, our boss, our peers and our stakeholders, regardless of any hierarchy.

We want to know that each of us has a voice and an opinion that is heard and valued.

Flattening workplace hierarchies has been a bit of a trend for several years. The argument for such a radical break from tradition is that so-called flat workplaces are more likely to spark collaborations and creative innovations.

Zappos have led the way in this area with their 'holacracy' initiative, a decentralised self-organisation structure that has no managers so as to limit bureaucracy and increase productivity and adaptability.

Yet it's not just employees who have different expectations when it comes to communication and connection; it is also our customers.

Once upon a time, we would wait until we had all the answers before we communicated what was going on (especially externally), but now the immediacy and urgency of social media means we can no longer afford to wait. Customers will be on Twitter to find out what is happening in real time. As an example of this, a few years ago when my husband, Steve, was the commercial property manager of Collins Place in Melbourne, a small fire broke out on the roof. Being surrounded by buildings full of city workers with a clear view, many of these people took photos and videos and uploaded them to Twitter. I saw these Tweets and called Steve to see if he knew about the fire... which he was unaware of.

Now this was just a minor incident of little consequence but it highlights how immediately communication can be spread. Within minutes of the fire starting, this information was on social media—and even before the key people in the company were aware of it.

The time of companies taking days or even hours to deliberate what should or shouldn't be communicated is over. They need to be more timely with their communication. Silence is dangerous.

Employees and customers respond to transparent and timely communication, as opposed to contrived and controlled communication.

Customers and employees expect to know what is going on and they expect to know now!

In-time communication

On a busy Saturday morning in 2018, the National Australia Bank's internet banking system and ATM and point of sale network went down. The media coverage of the outage was swift and relentless, rightly condemning the bank for the inconvenience to customers and the loss of revenue to merchants.

The communications on the day, however, were also swift and transparent from the senior leaders at the bank. Anthony Healy, Chief Customer Officer—Business & Private Banking, took to Twitter during the outage to apologise for the outage via a personal video he filmed at home.

A few weeks later, when everything had been resolved and it was no longer making news, Healy posted an article on LinkedIn that was noticeable for its personal and transparent nature. It read:

It started off much like every other Saturday morning.

A slower pace, a battle with the new coffee machine (one I am not winning!), kids getting ready for weekend sports and me reading the papers. And like many parents, Kate and I were gearing up for a couple of drop offs/pick ups as the kids went about doing their extra-curricular activities.

The day started off with best intentions.

Having lost the battle with the coffee machine, I headed out to the local café (long time NAB customers and lovely people) and like so many others who were doing similar things that crisp morning, when it came to paying for my two coffees...I couldn't.

'Our terminal isn't working, we don't know what is going on,' said the café owner, clearly confused. 'It's been like this for the last 15 mins. I'm sorry, but do you have cash on you?'

And with that comment, Saturday 26th May became not-so-typical. We had failed.

A quick check of my phone and numerous alerts from colleagues informed me that a series of failures originating from our power switching equipment had impacted our mainframe, causing a nationwide outage affecting ATMs, Internet Banking and EFTPOS terminals.

An incredibly rare event, but one that meant we were unable to get the core banking basics right for our customers on that morning.

Many will be familiar with the Greek philosophy that tells us 'it's not what happens to you, but how you react'. It's something that I try to live by, both professionally and personally, and when faced with the significant challenge on this cold Saturday morning, it was a philosophy I found our whole organisation had already put into gear.

Technicians were working to restore the systems, our call centre and branch staff were helping customers with workarounds and numerous other colleagues were on the phone discussing what we could do to demonstrate to our customers just how seriously we take incidents like this.

My job? Well, on this occasion I wanted to reassure our customers we were trying to make this right.

Expertly filmed in the hallway at home by my daughter and posted to Twitter, it was a simple message: we had failed in delivering the services we aspire to deliver and we were determined to right our wrong, including offering compensation to customers impacted by the outage.

Quickly, confidently and with determination, our people mobilised to help customers.

Since that Saturday thousands of NAB people, including the executive leadership team, have been on the phones or spoken to customers directly to apologise and work with them to organise compensation, which has now been paid to over 95% of customers who have contacted us.

Just as we said we would.

We know the impact of the outage on our customers was significant. And that's not acceptable to us.

But I'm proud of the way we have responded, which is what being more than money is all about.

Now there is no denying that the bank stuffed up. A six-hour outage to their entire system caused considerable inconvenience to their customers and merchants.

However, they were applauded for their response and willingness to take full responsibility, and for communicating that quickly and clearly.

That is what is required in today's communication world.

The communication conundrum

When it comes to what and when to communicate, the metric for risk needs to change if we want to satisfy our employees' and customers' need for connection and timely communication.

In the past, companies would be concerned about sharing too much information, when now they should be concerned about sharing too little.

Senior leaders, in particular, need to share what's going on in their business, and they need to be more accessible. Many CEOs now provide their direct email to employees and customers in case they need to contact them with issues.

We are seeing other examples of this increased connection and accessibility from senior leaders in organisations. Where CEO's or senior executives are frequently recording videos of themselves visiting customers and employees, and posting these directly onto social media channels such as Facebook and LinkedIn. Examples of this include Shayne Elliot, CEO of ANZ bank, Andy Penn, CEO of Telstra and Don Meij, CEO of Domino's Pizza.

In the past, leaders would not want to be seen as too familiar, but now the risk is being seen as elitist, or not relatable or approachable.

Large organisations are now talking about the need for their leaders to be 'more human', to be relaxed and natural when connecting with customers and employees, and to show and translate vulnerability.

Done authentically these kinds of interactions can build a real connection with employees and customers alike. When they're not authentic, however, they can backfire and just seem awkward for everyone involved. We've all seen too many examples of leaders (especially politicians) attempting to do this and ending up looking very stiff, awkward and totally inauthentic.

You want to avoid a scenario like that of Mr Burns on *The Simpsons* when he was encouraged to get out and speak to the workers. Bouncing up to an employee he obviously did not know the name of he said, 'Hey there, Mr Brown-shoes. How about that local sports team, eh?'

We want to know our leaders are not perfect and that they have experienced challenges and failures just like us.

Power employer to power employee

If you look closer in many workplaces, you will see that underlying power has shifted from employer to employee.

Many recruiters tell stories about how they felt they were the ones being interviewed by the potential candidate, not the other way around. One of my clients, who would be classified as gen Y, told me about being headhunted for a senior role, and insisting on meeting with the Executive General Manager, even though she would not be reporting to him. After the meeting, she turned down the role because she thought he didn't have any new ideas and displayed 'old-school' style leadership.

Businesses have no choice but to meet the evolving expectations of all their employees and customers, at all points of connection and communication, and regardless of their age or background, if they want to attract, retain and engage them.

CHAPTER 3
RISE OF JARGON

The first business book I ever really read cover to cover was *Watson's Dictionary of Weasel Words* by Don Watson.[1] It was gifted to me by a colleague (thanks, Catherine) when I left my corporate career.

Published in 2004, it contained an A to Z list of corporate jargon, which I loved and could relate to immediately. However, it was the opening paragraph that really got me:

> When the Prime Minister speaks of core and non-core election promises, your boss asks you to commit to an involuntary career event (you're fired), and hospitals refer to negative patient outcomes (you're dead), you know you are in a world gone mad. Politicians and managers not meaning what they say is nothing new, but these days it seems they are also incapable of saying what they mean. Groaning with platitudes and clichés, their words kill meaning and twist the truth. Spontaneity is rare, expressiveness and imagination long dead. It's time to fight back.

The issue is that we still seem to have the same issue. In fact, *Watson's Dictionary of Weasel Words* needs an updated edition to include all the

---

[1] There were many others that I had started but never completed.

corporate jargon, phrases and words that have emerged in the past decade and a half alone.

How often do you hear something like this in meetings?

> The optics will not be good on this project if we don't get all the ducks in a row and move the needle significantly enough to affect our employee value proposition. Let's marinate overnight, perhaps run it up the flagpole and revert back by close of play tomorrow.

The problem with jargon and clichés is that they seem really obvious when we're on the outside looking in. But they can seem to work just fine when we're on the inside of a certain group, not bothering to look up or out. Jargon comprises those terms and phrases that can feel like a shorthand concise language to people on the inside. They can make you feel like you're saying more with less (when often the opposite is true). Clichés might seem like the perfect way to describe or sum up a situation. They're usually the first thing to come to mind when you try to do so. But to people on the outside, jargon can make the conversation seem impenetrable while clichés make it trite, boring and obvious.

It's like we are talking in another language.

Are we on the same planet?

When I was working in Vietnam with a client, everyone in the client team spoke both English and Vietnamese. As I was facilitating the training, it was conducted in English (considering I couldn't speak Vietnamese).

At one point, we were having a break and I was involved in a small group conversation when two of the team members in the group starting talking to each other in their native language. One of the other leaders suggested that because I didn't know any Vietnamese they should all speak in English so I could hear and feel included.

Now not speaking a different language in front of someone who does not understand it might seem like a pretty obvious thing, but it's something that gets overlooked in business communications all the time when it comes to jargon.

When we use business jargon, we are effectively using another language that our audience might not understand.

We wouldn't speak Vietnamese in front of people who don't understand Vietnamese, so why use jargon in front of people who might not understand it?

It may not be as obvious that we are speaking a different language, but often we are. And that's not just rude; it can also cost us dearly when it comes to inclusivity, an important factor in determining team productivity.

Unless everyone in the conversation knows the literal translation of the word or phrase you are using, you are alienating certain people in that conversation.

The impact of technology

The increased availability and sophistication of technology is having a significant contribution to the increase of new words, phrases and jargon, which adds to the general feeling of confusion and sometimes overwhelm.

Take, for example, the increasing numbers of organisations that are adopting the 'agile' concept of working. This has a whole language of its own, with talk of squads, sprints and scrums.

In fact, the term has its own Wikipedia definition. First outlining how agile manufacturing is all about increasing an organisation's customer and marker response times while keeping on top of costs and quality, Wikipedia then offers this to (ahem) clarify:

> An enabling factor [...] has been the development of manufacturing support technology that allows the marketers, the designers and the production personnel to share a common database of parts and products, to share data on production capacities and problems—particularly where small initial problems may have larger downstream effects.

Now did you understand that? Wikipedia then compares agile manufacturing to lean manufacturing, using a quite neat analogy—lean manufacturing is like a thin person whereas agile manufacturing is more like an athletic person. And that analogy is the only part of the whole entry that really made sense to me! (This highlights the power of analogy and metaphor in good communication and storytelling—see chapter 6 for more.)

Cloud computing is no better. Again, Wikipedia is little help, describing it as an:

> Information technology (IT) paradigm that enables ubiquitous access to shared pools of configurable system resources and higher-level services that can be rapidly provisioned with minimal management effort, often over the Internet. Cloud computing relies on sharing of resources to achieve coherence and economies of scale, similar to a public utility.

These definitions make me feel even more stupid now I know I'm supposed to understand them. And as someone who worked in information technology for over 15 years that is saying something.

While these definitions are supposed to help clarify meaning for people, they actually end up doing the opposite.

Oops, we did it again

It's not only developing technology that is adding to our list of jargon. Often jargon is born from a simple comment or reference to something in a certain way (which normally is quite punchy...the first time it's said) and then all of a sudden, it's spreading around the office like wildfire.

For example, my younger daughter Jess once looked at the 'handy-man' hands of my husband, Steve, and said, 'Dad, you need a manicure, I will give you one'. Alex, my older daughter, chipped in with, 'And while we are at it, I will give you a facial because your skin is really oily'. I looked at him and said, 'This is an intervention'. Steve responded with 'What's an intervention? That's jargon'.

I thought everyone knew what 'an intervention' was, but apparently not. I explained to him that Alex and Jess believed that they needed to step in and help him with his beauty routine regardless of whether he realised it needed improvement or wanted it, so they were joining forces and intervening... an intervention. Alex then remarked that it was a 'skintervention' and there you go, more jargon was born!

In the future, when we say 'you need a skintervention' only the four of us will know exactly what it means because of our joint experience.[2]

I have seen this kind of process play out in the workplace on many occasions. For example, in one company that had adopted the agile manufacturing methodology, someone was complaining about another colleague who had said they were not implementing changes fast enough. With that another peer responded with, 'They are just agile shaming us'. The team loved it and started to use 'agile shaming' as a joke, but I noticed after time the terms had become part of their everyday language.

This is exactly the problem when it comes to business.

Teams have their own jargon. Companies and industries have their own jargon. Even countries have their own jargon.

Say that again

Babbel is one of the world's most popular learning language apps. In 2018, they asked representatives from international chambers of commerce in the United States about country-specific jargon and reported it in *Babbel* magazine.

Here are a few of the more unusual ones.

From Indonesia:

- Phrase: 'Asal bapak senang'

- Literal translation: 'Keeping Father happy'

- Meaning: Hiding bad news from the boss; being a 'yes-man'

Belgium:

- Phrase: 'De kogel is door de kerk'

- Translation: 'The bullet is through the church'

- Meaning: The decision has been made

---

[2] Well, except you now (and everyone else reading this) because I have just explained it to you.

The Netherlands:

- Phrase: 'Water naar de zee dragen'
- Literal translation: 'Carrying water to the sea'
- Meaning: A futile activity

France:

- Phrase: 'Avoir du pain sur la planche'
- Translation: 'To have bread on the cutting board'
- Meaning: We've got work to do

Germany:

- Phrase: 'Jetzt's geht's um die Wurst!'
- Translation: 'Now it is about the sausage!'
- Meaning: The final stages of a project/the moment when it counts

Greece:

- Phrase: 'του έψησε το ψάρι στα χείλη'
- Literal translation: 'He cooked the fish on his lips'
- Meaning: He made his life difficult

Norway:

- Phrase: 'Det gikk litt fort i svingene'
- Literal translation: 'The speed was too high in the turns'
- Meaning: Making mistakes by rushing to get a task done

Poland:

- Phrase: 'Co ma piernik do wiatraka?'
- Literal translation: 'What does gingerbread have to do with a windmill?'
- Meaning: What does one task have to do with another?

Sweden:

- Phrase: 'Glida in på en räkmacka'

- Literal translation: 'Sliding in on a shrimp sandwich'

- Meaning: To have things easy; to succeed without having to work hard

And don't even get me started on trying to understand teenagers. They are 'getting salty' and either 'throwing shade' or 'throwing hands'. Everything is lit or Gucci or Hundo P.[3]

So jargon can be specific to country, industry, company, team and generation.

It's no wonder that we feel overwhelmed and confused—and sometimes like we just don't fit in.

What are we hiding?

In the everyday business environment, jargon is often used in three unconscious—and also sometimes very deliberate—ways. It's used for:

1. acceptance

2. avoidance

3. importance.

The following sections look at each of these uses.

Acceptance

One of our greatest desires as humans is to be connected to each other and accepted, often at any cost. We act in a certain way to fit in. We dress in a certain way to fit in. We talk in a certain way to fit in.

All it takes is a senior person or an external consultant to start using a particular phrase and then, in most cases, gradually everyone else starts to use it.

---

[3] I was going to list some of the very latest teenage slang, but any list would be out of date before this book goes to print.

Have you ever played 'Buzzword Bingo' in meetings? You prepare bingo cards full of the latest jargon (or buzzwords) your boss, manager or colleagues love to throw around, and then tick them off when someone uses the word in a meeting or presentation. Not surprisingly, you might also know the game as 'Bullshit Bingo'.

I can recall when I changed positions in my early 30s and went to my first few meetings in my new role. I could not believe how many times I heard the word 'robust' used. Then a few years after that 'executional excellence' was the latest fad, before 'operational excellence' took over. Now it's about 'pivoting' — something that has no doubt crept in from the cool kids in the start-up world.

A lot of these phrases become popularised after being coined by authors and professional service firms; for example, management consulting firm McKinsey & Company created the term 'the war for talent' in 1997, meaning fight to attract and retain talented people. I'm sure you have heard this on numerous occasions in today's meetings or boardrooms.

The 'tipping point' is another example. The term was first used by Morton Grodzins to explain how continually adding a small amount of weight to a balanced object would cause the object to eventually but suddenly tip. Grodzins first used the term when he studied integrating American neighbourhoods in the early 1960s. He discovered that most of the white families remained in a particular neighbourhood as long as the comparative number of black families in the neighbourhood remained small. However, at a certain point (the tipping point), when 'one too many' black families arrived, the remaining white families would vacate in quick procession.

Malcolm Gladwell then popularised this term in his bestselling book *The Tipping Point: How Little Things Can Make a Big Difference* published in 2000. Gladwell expanded this idea of reaching critical mass or a particular threshold to examine a broad range of sociological changes — from sales of Hush Puppies shoes in the mid-1990s to the steep drop in New York City's crime rate after 1990.

This usage doesn't seem like a huge problem, until people start using it incorrectly.

A few months ago, I mistakenly used my daughter Jess's toothbrush. When she asked me about this, I dismissed it with, 'Sorry I didn't realise it was yours'. To which she replied, 'I would have thought my name on it[4] would have been the tipping point'. I could not resist pointing out to her that her usage of the term was incorrect (let alone that she had used it).

However, if people don't know exactly what a term means—but other people seem to use it a lot—then they start to use it incorrectly, like Jess did. Of course, they don't know they are using it incorrectly so they say it with confidence and they say it often. This alternative usage then moves around the office like Chinese whispers to the point where no shared understanding exists at all.

Avoidance

Sometimes people default to jargon when they have something to hide or they want to avoid the possibility of including (or evoking) any emotion in their communication.

We often see this when companies refer to cutting jobs (that is, making people unemployed) as 'downsizing' or 'rightsizing'. In December 2018, General Motors took this to a whole new level when they referred to the closure of five plants in the United States and Canada—with a loss of up to 14 000 jobs—as being unallocated. That's right—instead of saying words like 'sack', 'closure' or' job losses', they referred to these factories and people as 'unallocated'.

CEO Mary Barra used the term three times when speaking to market analysts, including in the statement, 'Market conditions require that five North American assembly and propulsion plants will be unallocated product by the end of 2019'.

Politicians are also very good at using jargon when they have something to hide and want to avoid answering a question with the truth.

Take the following example, which I first discussed in my book *Ignite* (published in 2015). This is an edited extract of an exchange between a journalist and Australia's then-immigration minister Scott Morrison

---

[4] Don't even ask why she put her name on her toothbrush. It didn't last long.

(subsequently elected leader of the Liberal Party and sworn in as Prime Minister in 2018).

> **Journalist:** Minister, is there a boat in trouble off Christmas Island?
>
> **Morrison:** It is our standard practice as you know, under Operation Sovereign Borders, to report on any significant events regarding maritime operations at sea, particularly where there are safety of life at sea issues associated, and I am advised I have no such reports to provide.
>
> **Journalist:** Is there a boat?
>
> **Morrison:** Well, I have answered the question.
>
> **Journalist:** ... So are you saying that boats are not leaving [for Australia]?
>
> **Morrison:** We are always ready for boats that may arrive and we always anticipate that they may seek to come and we are always ready. We are ready today, we were ready yesterday and we will be ready tomorrow and the government's policies will continue to prevail.
>
> **Journalist:** So Mr Morrison, you are not even going to confirm there is a boat; you are not going to say what is happening if people are in the water? Their boat is leaking, we are told — leaking oil — and you are not going to say anything about that situation?
>
> **Morrison:** What I have said is that it is our practice to report on significant events at sea, particularly when they involve safety of life at sea. Now there is no such report for me to provide to you today. If there was a significant event happening then I would be reporting on it.
>
> **Journalist:** So what does that mean?
>
> **Morrison:** You are a bright journalist. I'm sure you can work it out.
>
> **Journalist:** No, we are asking you, Sir. You are the minister.
>
> **Morrison:** And I have given you my response.
>
> **Journalist:** So could you clarify, Sir, for us — at what point does an event become a significant event involving a boat on the water?
>
> **Morrison:** When you see me here standing and reporting on it.
>
> **Journalist:** And you are standing here reporting.

Morrison: I am not. I am saying there is no such report for me to provide to you today. There is, therefore, no significant event for me to report at sea.

Journalist: Are you saying that it could be a hoax that people are saying they are in trouble?

Morrison: I am not saying anything of that at all. I am not confirming any of these matters. This should come as no surprise to you. This has been our practice now for the entire period of this operation. This is another day at the office for Operation Sovereign Borders.

It's infuriating, right?

In fact, a 2011 study at the New York University concluded that there was a lower level of trust when vague words were used (such as, 'An apology would be needed if my words have caused offence') and a higher level when more concrete words were used (such as, 'I am sorry').

We saw numerous examples of people using vague words and avoiding questions—of avoiding the truth—in the interviews conducted from Australia's 2017 royal commission into misconduct in the banking industry.

Following the commission, Don Watson, author of *Watson's Dictionary of Weasel Words* wrote a column 'A pack of bankers' in *The Monthly* in June 2018. The article focused on the senior executives who failed to take responsibility for what they had done and used language that watered down the seriousness of their actions. Watson concluded his article by arguing all the failures revealed by the royal commission were not caused by 'human bastardry or weakness' but by process. The article finishes with the following:

> [...] as with the industry, so with the regulator: all the processes were expressed in language so ingeniously meaningless, so calculated to disguise or make legitimate what was clearly illegitimate, they never used and never heard words, like 'swindle', 'dupe', 'cheat' or 'scam', that might have woken them to the truth.

We tend to use jargon when we want to avoid something but, ironically, the more you use jargon, the more people think you are just flat out lying.

Importance

I have a friend who, by her own admission, makes comments during football games that cite clichés she has no real understanding of. 'The third quarter is the premiership quarter'; 'anything can happen in finals'; 'it's not over till the fat lady starts singing'—that type of thing.

Initially, my friend sounds like she knows what she is talking about but as soon as the conversation moves away from the cliché commentary, it becomes clear she doesn't. As soon as someone asks a follow-up question, her cracks in knowledge start to appear. And, as I mentioned, my friend will put her hand up and admit that she uses these clichés to sound like she knows what's going on.

Believe it or not, research does show that using certain jargon and clichés does make us appear more credible (at least at first, and only in certain forums).

At the University of Munster, Germany, Dr Regina Jucks and Maria Zimmermann published 'How experts' use of medical technical jargon in different types of online health forums affects perceived information credibility: Randomised experiment with laypersons' (which is, ironically, an extremely long, jargon-filled title).

The objective of the research was to investigate how experts who use 'accommodative' versus 'non-accommodative' language are evaluated by people on an online forum. 'Non-accommodative' language was defined as language that contained high amounts of medical technical jargon.

Participants were split into groups where they were read online posts containing ten nutritional myths from experts. The posts were written using either a high level or a low level of jargon. The groups were then split into two. One group consisted of all medical experts, while the other consisted of laypersons. Participants then evaluated the credibility of the information and the trustworthiness of the communication.

The results showed that using high amounts of jargon when talking to other medical experts resulted in higher credibility than using less jargon in these forums. Conversely the opposite was true. For the layperson, using low amounts of jargon resulted in higher credibility than using high amounts of jargon. (Again, this relates back to being made to feel like the speaker is using a different language.)

However, in both situations, the more jargon was used the less it was perceived as trustworthy. I will talk more about this in chapter 9, but it highlights that when we overuse jargon, people trust us less and doubt our intentions.

In business, individuals may purposely use jargon, knowing that it is confusing for their clients.

The end result is that clients may feel like they have no choice but to engage these people in their service because it just sounds too confusing to not have their help. However, when jargon is used deliberately like this it can ultimately lead to distrust and clients will end up going elsewhere.

We also often use jargon and more 'sophisticated' or unfamiliar language to impress others but this can backfire. My husband, Steve, loves to use big words. He would often use big words and then jokingly say to me, 'You don't know what that means do you?' and I would reply 'No, I don't and you know I don't, which makes you a shit communicator'. Boom! He may be smart but I am a better smartarse.

It can also backfire when our grasp on language isn't as strong as it could be or we get nervous or flustered. (Perhaps you remember Tony Abbott's 'suppository of all wisdom' gaffe from 2013.) Again, these attempts to look smart can have the exact opposite effect.

However, you will perhaps see no greater example of jargon used to impress others than when you look at job titles.

In 2017, Forbes listed '20 ridiculous job titles that make even the most boring jobs sound thrilling' and they included:

- *Galactic Viceroy of Research Excellence at Microsoft:* This was assigned to someone who did cloud-related research.

- *Dean of Pizza at Pizza Hut:* This role required training Pizza Hut managers on how to properly cut and place the pizza in the box.

- *Director of Sound Design at Facebook:* Responsible for creating all the 'pop ding' and 'pop om' sounds you hear when you receive a notification on your Facebook feed.

- *Executive Sensei at Virginia Mason Medical:* Helps support clients and manage the business aspects of the company.

- *In-House Philosopher at Google:* Responsible for solving engineering problems using a 'humanistic perspective'.

If those job titles are not bizarre enough, what about the increase of 'chiefs' occurring these days. There was once a time when a business had only a Chief Executive Officer and maybe a Chief Financial Officer. Now it seems the list is endless, including:

- Chief Information Officer

- Chief Risk Officer

- Chief Operating Officer

- Chief People Officer

- Chief Marketing Officer.

Some unique ones I have spotted on LinkedIn include:

- Chief Digital Inspiration Officer

- Chief Fixed Officer

- Chief Experience Officer

- Chief Creative Officer

- Chief Edge Officer.

Though my star picks for the most bizarre are:

- Chief Wine Hacker

- Chief Troublemaker

- Chief Executive Unicorn.

Any of these jobs sound good.

> *They also, in most cases, make the role sound more important than perhaps the actual job is and involves.*

Is it ever acceptable to use jargon?

While most jargon is confusing and misleading, it's not all bad.

When used correctly, jargon can be an efficient and accurate way of communicating—IF (a very big IF) everyone fully understands what it means.

If you are presenting a highly technical topic to a group of highly technical people (such as doctors presenting to doctors or lawyers to lawyers) who will understand your use of technical jargon, it may be acceptable. If you are presenting highly technical information to people who don't understand the topic or the language commonly associated with it (such as doctors presenting to patients or lawyers to clients), you need to reduce the jargon or explain what it means.

As we just explored, using jargon can become inefficient and inaccurate very quickly if it is not understood or is misconstrued.

Here are some more examples of when it is okay or not okay to use jargon to help you think this through.

Is it acceptable to use the phrase 'move the needle' at work?

Are you a seamstress or a doctor or a DJ?

- *Yes:* It's acceptable.

- *No:* Stop using it. Try saying something like, 'We need to do something that will make a visible difference'.

Is it acceptable to use the phrase 'think outside the square' at work?

Are you trying to show you are innovative by using a phrase coined in the 1970s?

- *Yes:* Go for it.

- *No:* Stop using it. Try saying, 'We need to do something different'.

Is it acceptable to use the term 'buy-in' at work?

Are you purchasing shares in a company?

- *Yes:* It's acceptable.

- *No:* Don't use it. Try 'support' instead.

Is it acceptable to use the word 'marinate' at work?

Are you a chef?

- *Yes:* It's acceptable.

- *No:* Don't use it. Replace it with 'let me think about it'.

Is it acceptable to use the phrase 'singing from the same hymn sheet' at work?

Are you in a church choir?

- *Yes:* It's acceptable.

- *No:* Stop using it. Say something like, 'Do we all understand what needs to be done?' instead.

Is it acceptable to use the phrase 'we don't need to boil the ocean' at work?

Do you have a saucepan big enough to make this possible?

- *Yes:* It's acceptable

- *No:* Don't use it. Try just saying, 'We don't need to make this more difficult than it needs to be'.

It is acceptable to use jargon if you are sure EVERYONE in the conversation or who you are communicating to fully understands it.

The real issue is that this level of understanding is very rare! So tread lightly.

CHAPTER 4

ADDICTION TO ACRONYMS

I started my career in IT at NAB, as a TCO in FES, which looked after NAB's ATM and POS network.

Did you understand that sentence? My guess is, no. You may have deciphered some of those acronyms and abbreviations, but probably not all of them.

Now, let me rephrase it without all the shorthand: I started my career in information technology at National Australia Bank, as a trainee computer operator in front-end systems, which looked after National Australia Bank's automatic teller machines and point of sale network.

Which is easier to understand? The second explanation without acronyms, I expect.

A lot of acronyms we are familiar with today start in a technical environment such as information technology (or IT).

In the early years of my work in technology, for example, everything was about RAM (random-access memory) and DOS (disk operating system).

Then we moved to Y2K — remember that? — the Year2000 bug or millennium bug, a coding problem that was projected to create havoc in computer networks all around the world at the beginning of the year 2000. That amounted to, well, nothing.

After this, projects all became about implementing SAP (systems applications products) and LMS (learning management systems). Now we have CX (customer experience), UX (user experience) and even EX (employee experience).

The list of acronyms, abbreviations and initialisms never ends! It's confusing and at times overwhelming.

In fact, let's explore what we mean by acronyms, abbreviations and initialisms, because their definitions are just as bad:

- *Acronym:* An abbreviation formed from the initial letters of other words and pronounced as a word (for example, AIDS, or acquired immune deficiency syndrome).

- *Abbreviation:* A shortened form of a word or phrase (for example, Dr, short for doctor).

- *Initialism:* An abbreviation consisting of initial letters pronounced separately (for example, BBC, or British Broadcasting Corporation).

So, acronyms are abbreviations that can be pronounced as words, and initialisms are abbreviations that cannot be pronounced as words. Got it? I know — complicated, right? So for ease of use from now on, let's refer to them all collectively as acronyms.

More importantly, let's look at how they've crept into our world.

Acronyms for ease and efficiency

One of the main reasons we create acronyms is to make communication efficient and easier. For example, ATM (automatic teller machine) and PIN (personal identification number) were extremely new technical terms about 30 years ago, but today they are part of our everyday language, which pretty much most of us understand.

Scuba is another example. An acronym meaning self-contained underwater breathing apparatus, in 1952 it was not an official word but, sometime later, scuba made it into the Oxford English Dictionary. So too the word laser, which is an acronym of light amplification by stimulated emission of radiation

Examples like scuba and ATM have actually made communicating about the topics they relate to way more efficient. I mean, imagine being a diver and having to say 'self-contained underwater breathing apparatus' every time you were referring to your gear — you would be out of oxygen before you knew it.

Gradually with time, acronyms can become accepted into language, and you may not even realise they started life as an acronym.

What the acronym stands for actually becomes less relevant.

Take the term 'care package' as another example. This is now understood as something you send someone to show them you care and, like scuba and laser, it started life as an acronym. After World War II, packages were sent via the Cooperative for American Remittances to Europe (CARE) to American relatives living in Europe who were struggling in the aftermath of war. The organisation later changed its name to Cooperative for Assistance and Relief Everywhere (still CARE), and they began to distribute packages on a wider scale. Now, a care package can come from anyone and be sent to anyone.

SMART car is also an acronym meaning Swatch Mercedes ART. The story goes that these cars were developed by Swatch and brought to the market in partnership with Mercedes-Benz. The term was a compromise between the two companies' names.

It is also common practice to use acronyms to abbreviate the names of organisations. Some of today's most recognisable include:

- *QANTAS:* Queensland and Northern Territory Aerial Services

- *NASA:* National Aeronautics and Space Administration

- *FBI:* Federal Bureau of Investigation

- *UN:* United Nations

- *AT&T:* American Telephone and Telegraph Company

- *H&M:* Hennes and Mauritz

- *TED:* Technology, Entertainment, Design.

This trend does not seem to be stopping.

Ernst & Young was so-named after the two men who founded it, but in 2013 they started referring to themselves as EY. KPMG was formally KPMG Peat Marwick until 1999, and PricewaterhouseCoopers abbreviated their company name to PwC in 2011.

Will Deloitte follow suit and soon be known as D, I wonder?

You may not even realise some company names are abbreviations—for example, IKEA. The Swedish company takes its name from its founder's initials, Ingvar Kamprad, combined with the first initial of the farm where he grew up, Elmtaryd, and the parish he calls home, Agunnaryd.

WTF are you talking about?

Like jargon, using acronyms can be an efficient way to communicate *IF* everyone understands what they mean.

I recall once having a conversation with someone when they mentioned their challenge when dealing with SMEs. I automatically assumed she was referring to subject matter experts. The conversation became increasingly confusing for both of us until I clarified what she meant by SMEs. She was actually referring to small to medium enterprises.

Two people in the conversation can have two different understandings of the acronym, depending on the context, company or industry.

Another example of acronym confusion was when I received an email from my financial planner about my investment and she mentioned BPS. Having a technology background, I immediately interpreted that as bits per second, but I asked her to clarify just in case. It was a good job I did because it referred to basis points (which proves you can even translate two words into a three-letter acronym).[1]

While researching for this book, I spent a lot of time looking through the Oxford English Dictionary, which is often abbreviated to OED. In addition, I came across a list of 25 different versions of what OED can stand for.

LOL is another classic example of acronyms referring to more than one thing. To some it means laugh out loud and to others it means lots of love. Now imagine you only know LOL as meaning laugh out loud and your friend only knows it as meaning lots of love. And imagine you receive a text from your friend saying, 'I'm really sorry to hear that your dog died. LOL'. It could be the end of your friendship.

Some other common acronyms that have different meanings are:

- *AI*: Artificial intelligence versus augmented intelligence

- *STI*: Short term incentive versus sexually transmissible (or transmitted) infection

- *IP*: Intellectual property versus internet protocol.

Unless everyone around the table has the same meaning and understanding of the acronym, then miscommunication becomes more possible.

Deciding if people will understand the acronym is a judgement call and, unfortunately, we are often blinded by our own knowledge.

Curse of knowledge

The 'curse of knowledge' can be understood as a cognitive bias that occurs when an individual, communicating with others, unconsciously assumes that the recipient has the required background knowledge to understand the messages (that is, the same background knowledge as them).

In 1990, Elizabeth Newton, a student at Stanford University, conducted an experiment that demonstrated the curse of knowledge. A group of people were

[1] Of course, BPS can also refer to battered person's syndrome or bladder pain syndrome and a whole lot more.

asked to tap out well-known songs with their fingers, while another group tried to guess the songs. When the tappers were asked to predict how many songs they thought the listeners would guess correctly, they said about 50 per cent. The actual figure was 2.5 per cent. The tappers were so familiar with what they were tapping that they assumed listeners would easily recognise the song.

I have undertaken my own version of this experiment in some of my workshops. The tappers always say they feel frustrated when the listener cannot guess the song. What they are communicating seems so simple and logical to them that they become frustrated when the listener cannot guess it. The listeners also report feelings of frustration and, in some cases, of stupidity for not knowing the right song.

You may have also experienced the same thing when playing charades or Pictionary. It's annoying when you are acting out or drawing something completely obvious to you that the other person still cannot guess. (So you repeat the same action more vigorously or circle and underline your drawing as if that will help.)

I believe the curse of knowledge plays a big part in the overuse of acronyms. Where the communicator assumes that the recipient will know the term—because they themselves know them so well—the acronyms almost become invisible to the communicator, to the point they are probably unaware they are using them.

Ironically, the overuse of acronyms is now making communication harder and miscommunication easier.

Unnecessary acronym use (UAU)[2]

So acronyms can have a purpose and be efficient if used correctly; however, the problem is we now abbreviate pretty much anything and everything we can.

While at lunch with a friend once I asked the waiter what white wine they had by the glass. She replied with, 'We have an SB or SBS'. I sort of thought I knew what she meant but wasn't totally sure so I decided I would subtly make my point and ask her to explain what SB and SBS meant. As suspected, it was sauvignon blanc and sauvignon blanc semillon.

[2] You get that my reducing unnecessary acronym use to UAU is a joke, right?

I am sure I was not the first (or last) person to need to ask for an explanation—which means she had to stop and explain. If jargon and acronyms are used for efficiency and accuracy, surely it would be just more efficient and accurate for her to not reduce the wine types to acronyms.

We now create acronyms for acronyms' sake, and incorporate them into daily use like everyone knows what they mean.

I see an increase in unnecessary acronyms, driven mainly by companies with guidelines such as documents can only be two pages long or presentations four slides in length. The result? People use a smaller, less legible font, or include unnecessary acronyms to save on space.

For example, I once had a client show me a document that detailed the skills, knowledge and experience required for a particular position. But 'skills, knowledge and experience' had been abbreviated to SKE. Like, seriously. It became quite annoying to read because every time I read the abbreviation, I had to remind myself what SKE stood for.

So, as a communicator, it takes you less time to hit the required keys (in this example, S-K-E) on the keyboard, as opposed to having the extra burden of typing the whole phrase out. Yet, think of the time this wastes for the person you were communicating with (in this case, me) to have to then try to figure out what you meant.

You are putting all the onus and hard work on the reader to interpret what you are communicating.

Another company I know refers to their employees as EEs (yes, meaning employees) both in the written and spoken format. Surely, we don't need to reduce this word (and concept) to an acronym?

I once did some work for a company that had a database containing all their acronyms and there were more than 2500 entries. This is enough to give any new recruit nightmares! I did not even dare ask what this database was called because I just knew that too would be an acronym—the ADB (acronym data base), perhaps.

Just plain lazy

Put bluntly, using too many acronyms is just lazy and results in poor communication. For example, I am part of a mentoring program that is called the Women Athletes Business Network (WABN), but when people refer to it, they don't say the letters of the acronym separately (W A B N); they pronounce it wa-ben. Like it's a real word.

The issue is compounded when we pronounce acronyms as words when they are not actually existing words (or sound remotely like them).

Subject matter expert (SME) is another acronym that people often pronounce as 'smee' like it's a word. If the acronym actually sounds like a word, such as PIN, then it's acceptable to say the acronym as a word — but 'smee' and 'waben' don't sound anything like real words.

Sometimes, we even believe words were originally acronyms when no evidence supports it. An example of this, which I believed up until researching for this book, was 'posh'. Like me, you might have heard that the word 'posh' was originally an acronym for 'port over (or out), starboard home' — and the four letters referring to these words would be placed on affluent people's luggage on ships so they were allocated the best cabins. Extensive research by the Oxford English Dictionary has found no evidence to support this suggestion.

Of course, a word has been coined to describe this process and it's called a 'backronym'. (I kid you not.)

Is it ever okay, OK or K[3] to use acronyms?

I am the founder of Jargon Free Fridays and I must admit when I am sending emails to my executive manager about Jargon Free Fridays I often write JFF. Internally, this is acceptable. We both know what the acronym means and its use becomes an efficient way to communicate.

[3] Teenagers have managed to reduce OK to K. I'm not sure what comes after that.

The problem, however, is if we ever start to use this acronym outside of our very small team and with people who have absolutely no idea what we're referring to.

If the acronym is common knowledge to the people you are writing or talking to, generally it is acceptable to use it.

Like jargon, using acronyms may be wise in some situations. If you are going for a job interview or pitching for work and the potential employee or client is using a lot of acronyms, you may want to match their use of acronyms. However, you could also ask something like, 'When you say SME, are you referring to subject matter expert or small to medium enterprise?' to ensure you're referring to the same thing.

It may also be acceptable to use commonly known acronyms in an extensive written report if you're following the academic (and other published material) protocol of writing the phrase, term or name out in full the first time you use it and then inserting the acronym in brackets—for example, 'tax file number (TFN)'. For each subsequent mention, you can then just use the acronym.

But if you are only using the term a few times over the whole report, do you really need to reduce it to an acronym?

Most importantly, make sure the use of internal acronyms does not become part of the conversation with external customers, because that is what leads to miscommunication and inefficiency.

PART II

How we
get Real
Engagement

One of the best ways to increase engagement with our people is to communicate with them in a more genuine way.

As Richard Branson, my (and maybe your) business idol when it comes to authentic leadership, is quoted on his website as saying:

> Communication is not just about speaking or reading, but understanding what is being said—and in some cases what is not being said [...] It facilitates human connections, and allows us to learn, grow and progress. Master the art of communication and you'll experience great success in all aspects of life.

Communication is the most important skill any leader can possess. So in this section on Real Engagement, we will explore four ways to help you communicate more effectively. They are:

1. *Communicate concisely:* Too often when we communicate, we focus on ourselves and not on the people we are communicating with. However, it really pays to put your audience first and think of their needs, and what they want or need to hear from you.

2. *Share personal stories:* 'Just give me the facts!' is a phrase often heard throughout the corridors of organisations. However, when we focus on logic alone and dismiss emotion when we communicate, especially when we are trying to influence, our message rarely lands well. We need a balance of stories and facts to communicate our ideas.

3. *Visualise information:* We often underestimate the important role visual communication plays. This relates to how we make our content stand out and be more easily understood. As you will see, improving your visual content goes way beyond providing a list of bullet points on boring PowerPoint slides.

4. *Deliver your content with impact:* We often stumble at the final communication hurdle: delivering our content. Our doubts and fears creep in, which severely impacts how we stand up, show up, speak and deliver. Well, no more!

The chapters in this part are designed to provide you with some practical tools and techniques to apply and try out, whether you're preparing to speak on stage to a large audience, one-on-one with a customer, or even writing to your team.

CHAPTER 5

COMMUNICATE CONCISELY

How many meetings do you go to where you wonder why you are there? How many briefings or updates do you attend that could have been covered with a short email or phone call instead? How many emails do you receive that take six read-throughs to understand? How many presentations do you sit bored through because the speaker didn't address your needs?

Too many to count, right? I am sure you have experienced most of these situations before. They feel like a complete waste of time because, well, they are.

I see this time wasting happen a lot in organisations when the person conducting the meeting, sending the email or delivering the presentation has not put in the right effort to ensure the content is valuable for the people receiving the information.

This lack of effort is not only a waste of time; in business it's also a waste of money.

If a leader brings together 1000 people for a one-hour update, but doesn't prepare sufficiently enough or think about what they are communicating and why, what is the total business cost of that wasted time? For simplicity, let's just say each person attending the meeting earns $50 an hour. That means the organisation has wasted $50 000 for an update that no-one gets or understands.

When people give their time to come and hear you speak, you must make sure it is worth their while, as well as yours. Otherwise, what is the point?

One of the major reasons we don't communicate concisely is that we put ourselves first, instead of our audience.

Get your message write[1]

'If I had more time, I would have written a shorter letter' is a quote often incorrectly attributed to Mark Twain but was first used in 1657 by the French mathematician and philosopher Blaise Pascal. In Pascal's *Lettres Provinciales* he wrote in French:

> Je n'ai fait celle-ci plus longue que parce que je n'ai pas eu le loisir de la faire plus courte.

This roughly translates as, 'I have made this longer than usual because I have not had time to make it shorter'.

That pretty much sums up most of our written communication these days, especially when it comes to emails!

We're so busy punching out information on the keys that rarely do we stop and assess:

1. what the main message of the email is supposed to be

2. why the intended recipient needs to know

3. what you want them to do as a result.

The communication usually ends up as verbal diarrhoea (well written), which, in a lot of cases, then results in more back and forth emails between the sender and recipient as they try to work out what was meant by the first message.

[1] A deliberate pun, in case you were wondering.

This is so far from real communication, it's not funny!

Communicating this way is quite disrespectful to your intended recipient because (as when using jargon and acronyms—see the previous two chapters) you are putting the onus on them to do all the hard work. You should aim to minimise the effort and time required for the recipient to understand and respond to your message, even if that means more effort and time from you.

Chris Anderson and Jane Wulf from TED agree. In 2011, they wrote a blog post about the need for an email charter. They had so many hits, responses and comments on this post that they took it a step further. Together, they created the website emailcharter.org, which lists ten 'rules' to save our inboxes—with 'respect recipients' time' as their number 1 rule.

Ways you can respect your recipients' time and communicate more concisely include:

- Ensure the subject line clearly states the topic of the email and, if an action is required, this action is clearly stated.

- Don't unnecessarily CC people into emails. I worked with one manager who never read emails he was CCed in, saying that if the sender wanted him to read the email, they should send it directly to him.

- Don't unnecessarily 'reply all' when several people have been CCed in. Check who actually needs to see your response, and only include them.

- If someone introduces you to someone else (because the other person is better placed to help you) move the introducer to BCC for the initial response email with a comment like, 'Thank you for the introduction; [insert name] moved to BCC'. The introducer does not have to be CCed in all your ongoing emails with the other person.

The biggest problem, according to emailcharter.org, is 'the average time taken to respond to an email is greater, in aggregate, than the time it took to create'.

One great suggestion in Anderson and Wulf's charter is to 'Give these Gifts: EOM NNTR'. The authors suggest that if your message is only a few words then simply put those words in the subject line, followed by EOM (which equals 'end of message'). This saves the recipient time because they do not even have to open the email.

They also suggest that ending an email with NNTR (no need to respond) is a 'wonderful act of generosity'. (And this works both ways—how many times have you opened an email to see it only contains a quick 'Thanks for your help!'?) As you have probably gathered by now, I am not a fan of unnecessary acronyms but I think exceptions always exist to any rule and even I agree these are good acronyms we could adopt.

Stop wasting words

This concept that we're all too 'wordy' and wasting air time waffling instead of getting to the point is actually not new.

Long before Anderson and Wulf created the charter discussed in the previous section, others tried to do something similar, including England's Winston Churchill, Prime Minister of the United Kingdom from 1940 to 1945 and 1951 to 1955.

On 9 August 1940, during the Battle of Britain, Churchill asked his staff to write more concise reports. His memo stated:

> To do our work, we all have to read a mass of papers. Nearly all of them are far too long. This wastes time, while energy has to be spent in looking for the essential points.
>
> I ask my colleagues and their staffs to see to it that their Reports are shorter.
>
> 1. The aim should be Reports which set out the main points in a series of short, crisp paragraphs.
>
> 2. If the Report relies on detailed analysis of some complicated factors, or statistics, these should be set out in an Appendix.
>
> 3. Often the occasion is best met by submitting not a full-dress Report, but an *Aide-memoire* consisting of headings only, which can be expanded orally if needed.

4. Let us have an end to such phrases as these: 'It is also of importance to bear in mind the following considerations...', or 'Consideration should be given to the possibility of carrying into effect...'. Most of these wholly phrases are mere padding, which can be left out altogether or replaced by a single word. Let us not shrink for using the short expressive phrase, even if it is conversational.

Reports drawn up on the lines I propose may at first seem rough as compared with the flat surface of officialese jargon. But the saving in time will be great, while the discipline of setting out the real points concisely will prove an aid to clearer thinking.

My favourite quote in the memo is, 'the flat surface of officialese jargon'. (I think Winston Churchill would make a great ambassador for Jargon Free Fridays.)

So next time you send an email or write a report, just think: could I cut down this communication, make it shorter or the point clearer—or even not send it at all?

Meet me on time (and make it worth my while)

Meetings, done well, are an important source of communication and increase engagement. But put your hand up if you feel like you have meetings just for the sake of having meetings? Well, you are not alone.

A 2017 Harvard survey of 182 senior managers from different industries found that:

- 33 per cent of meetings are actually useful or purposeful

- 71 per cent of managers said meetings are unproductive and inefficient

- 62 per cent said meetings miss opportunities to bring teams closer together.

Does that sound like engaging communication to you?

In fact, I know someone who took over scheduling a weekly meeting with stakeholders. After a while, she realised that nothing was really happening in the actual meeting—nothing was decided or acted on. As an experiment, she simply stopped scheduling the meetings to see what would happen. Not one person asked why they were not happening or asked for them to resume.

The issue is that meetings (like email) have become a default communication tool.

In Donna McGeorge's book *The 25 Minute Meeting*, she explains that most of us use a calendar app that defaults our meetings to 60 minutes, so somewhere along the way our brain has defaulted to this setting too.

We schedule meetings for 60 minutes when, in fact, we can double our impact in the less than half the time just by cutting meetings down to 25 minutes.

McGeorge explains that we are actually cushioning our meetings with extra fat—that is, a whole bunch of unnecessary time and waffle. She says:

> Our bad meeting habits are costing us:
>
> - waiting for latecomers: (at least) 5 minutes
>
> - wondering about the agenda: 5 minutes
>
> - waffling and going off track: 5 minutes
>
> - watching mobile phones or PCs: 5 minutes
>
> - wasting time on fixing tech: 5 minutes.
>
> There's 25 minutes RIGHT THERE that you could recover if you got rid of bad meeting habits, and I think I've been generous with time. We frequently spend more than 5 minutes on some of these things.

The key take outs from this book are that you can make your meetings more effective, and your overall communication land with more impact using some really simple methods. These include:

1. Inviting only those people who really need to be there (stop CCing absolutely everyone!)

2. Attending only if you really need to be there (determine your role in the meeting)

3. Ensuring the meeting has a clear purpose (identify the intended outcome)

4. Preparing an agenda for everyone ahead of time (set expectations)

5. Arriving on time (be prepared to contribute)

6. Starting on time (avoid waiting for latecomers)

7. Finishing on time (be respectful of everyone there).

If your meeting does go over time, make sure everyone is okay with that. I was privy to a meeting once where the senior executive asked for everyone's approval to go 10 minutes more. Once confirmed, she asked if anyone had another meeting to go and, if so, if they needed to text someone from the next meeting to let them know they would be late.

That is how you keep meetings real.

Be present when you present

I was once told a horror story about a trainer who ran a session on executive presence for senior women at a global professional service firm. While some of the content provided was useful, much of it was completely inappropriate and old-school.

When the trainer got to the point of telling the women how to dress—for example, to wear a certain type of blazer and not cardigans—the room started to voice their concerns. One of the participants suggested to the trainer that, 'We don't need to hear this; we all know how to dress'. She responded with, 'You do need to hear this'.

The more inappropriate the things the woman suggested, such as 'don't talk about your children at work', the more the participants started to disengage. Unfortunately, this trainer was not reading the room at all and continued on—until she started showing them how to do a 'proper handshake'. At this point, the participants turned on her, took control and literally asked her to leave and not return.

Being able to contribute and present to an audience is part and parcel of any job, whether we are a leader, a trainer or otherwise. You might need to deliver a pitch to your small team of colleagues or customers, for example, or present a new strategy at a larger event.

Most of us are so focused on our own agenda or outcome that we fail to think of our audience and their unique situation and needs.

Whatever way you present, you need to respect three areas when you are speaking to a room of people:

1. time

2. situation

3. culture.

Respect participants' time

Believe it or not, some of the world's most renowned speeches have lasted no longer than 20 minutes:

- *Martin Luther King's 'I have a dream':* 17 minutes

- *Steve Jobs' 'Stay hungry, stay foolish':* 15 minutes

- *Winston Churchill's 'Never give up':* 4 minutes

I wonder if we would have enjoyed these speeches or been as engaged by them if they had waffled on for 50 or 60 minutes.

Nope, I doubt it, too.

The highly successful TED Talk imposes a strict rule of no longer than 18 minutes, regardless of whether you are Bill Clinton or Bono, for a reason. Chris Anderson, the head of TED, is quoted in Carmille Gallo's book, *Talk Like TED*, as saying:

❝ It [18 minutes] is long enough to be serious and short enough to hold people's attention. It turns out that this length also works incredibly well online. It's the length of a coffee break. So, you watch a great talk, and forward the link to two or three people. It can go viral, very easily. The 18-minute length also works much like the way Twitter forces people to be disciplined in what they write. By forcing speakers who are used to going on for 45 minutes to bring it down to 18, you get them to really think about what they want to say. What is the key point they want to communicate? It has a clarifying effect. It brings discipline.

The reality is that the more time you spend talking, the more time you spend waffling and confusing your audience.

These days, we are competing for our audience's attention against an influx of information. It's estimated that the average person makes about 35 000 semi-conscious decisions each day. We need to be able to communicate clearly and concisely so we can get to our main message quickly and with ease, before decision fatigue sets in, or we lose everyone's focus.

This is easier said than done, of course. The reality is that it is harder to prepare for a shorter speech than a longer one. (Just as it's harder to write a shorter email than a longer one.)

I know from my own experience that the shorter the speech I am asked to give, the more time I have to prepare for it. And this is backed up by a reported quote from Woodrow Wilson (no less!), the 28th President of the United States of America. When asked in 1919 how long he spent preparing his speeches, Woodrow is reported to have responded:

❝ That depends on the length of the speech. If it is a ten-minute speech it takes me all of two weeks to prepare it; if it is a half-hour speech it takes me a week; if I can talk as long as I want to it requires no preparation at all. I am ready now.

When preparing for a shorter speech, I suggest you be very clear on what the purpose of your presentation is. Is the purpose to ask for resources? Is it to get people to donate their time or money? Is it to inspire people? Is it to simply inform people? Are you opening a conference and you need to set up the context of the day? Whatever the purpose of your presentation is, make sure you are very clear on this—and stick to that. Staying on point is always important, regardless of time, but this is critical the shorter time you have.

Too often when we give presentations we try to put too much information and messages into the talk. Be disciplined about the key message you need to get across. You don't need to include every message you would like your audience to know but only the critical ones they need to hear. Focus on one to three points, rather than eight to ten.

Do all the preparation work first. Make sure you practise so you are within the time limit. In most cases when you practise, because you are reading your speech it will take less time than when you actually deliver it for real (hopefully not reading). However, if you do the work beforehand with discipline, you won't feel the need to speak ridiculously fast on the day or, worse, go extremely over time.

Respect their situation

I was once presenting in Sydney with the magnificent Sydney Harbour (and Sydney Harbour Bridge) as the backdrop. At one point, I noticed all 200 audience members suddenly divert their gaze to the window behind me. I stopped talking, looked around and noticed a superb old sailing ship passing by. It was a spectacular sight as it made its way under the bridge.

So rather than compete with that, I got everyone to pause for a minute to watch the ship sail by, commenting on its grandeur. Once it had sailed out of sight, I turned back to the crowd and said, 'Now, where were we?' before continuing on.

When you're presenting, you need to be aware of what is happening in that situation, in that very moment. Sometimes, this just means being a bit flexible to ensure you get the most engagement but, at other times, it means being mindful of something that might be deemed insensitive.

For example, it doesn't matter how important your message is or what your agenda is, if your audience has just been informed a large proportion of them will soon lose their jobs, or some other terrible scenario, then you need to take that into account.

Many times I have been to a training session or a sales meeting with an organisation that has just announced significant restructures and job losses. If I hadn't allowed space for the resulting discussion to take place, there would have been very little engagement in what I was presenting.

Remember you are dealing with real humans, and if they have just received bad news about their job or they are going through significant disruption, your message may not be that important to them. You will come across as being more real and genuinely caring if you are flexible enough to ditch what you were going to say (or at least hold off on presenting it) and so create time for them to get things off their chest first.

Dismissing their feelings or making light of them or the situation so you can turn the focus back to you and get on with your presentation is not being real.

When you are faced with challenges that can affect communication, just embrace them and be real.

Respect their culture

Ten years ago, I ran some training for a global logistics company in Indonesia. At the start of the session, the host handed out gifts—traditional caps for the men and traditional wrap skirts for the women. The entire team was male and I was the only female and the facilitator for the day.

As the men put the caps on their head, I folded my skirt and placed it on the floor next to my bag. I then went on and delivered the training.

A few weeks later I caught up with the Managing Director, who was based in my home town of Melbourne. He informed me that my gesture of placing the skirt on the floor was taken as a massive insult to the hosts. I was mortified that I had offended them! I literally had no idea!

This is an all-too-common scenario when we are dealing or presenting to different cultures. And while it may be impossible to be across all cultural sensitivities, doing some research and asking some people who know the culture well what you should be aware of can be worthwhile. Ideally, if the experts you ask know you well, they could offer you some specific insights such as, 'You know how you often swear...well, don't'. If possible, also observe what other speakers are doing on the day.

We live in a multicultural world, with multiple languages, multiple definitions and multiple ways of miscommunicating.

The simple fact is that something you do or say can be totally misunderstood and cause havoc when it comes to real communication.

Our teams, customers, clients and stakeholders comprise different generations and different cultures, which means different ways of understanding the same piece of information.

You will be better at communicating more concisely if you put your audience's needs above yours.

Regardless of how you are communicating (written or spoken), when you consider your audience first, you ensure your message is concise, valuable and engaging.

Get REAL now

- Consider adopting the lessons provided at emailcharter.org.
- Arrive at, start and finish meetings on time.
- Only invite people to meetings who need to be there.
- Respect everyone's time, situation and culture.
- Read the room and know when to be flexible.
- Put your audience first to make sure your communication (spoken or written) is worth the time of the person receiving it.

CHAPTER 6

SHARE PERSONAL STORIES

About ten years ago, I was running a workshop for a senior leadership team. I was told that the CEO was sceptical about the power of storytelling in business, but she eventually agreed to the workshop.

It became clear within minutes that the whole organisation was suffering within a toxic culture. In over 35 years of working in business, I have never seen such bullying by anyone, let alone the CEO to her direct reports. It was an environment of intimidation and fear, and was extremely unpleasant to witness as a facilitator.

At one point the CEO's aggression moved from her team to me. She crossed her arms in a show of disdain for everything I was saying, and declared she had no need to learn how to use stories to communicate. She wanted the facts and figures, and not anything else. She challenged me that if I could not provide her with one valid reason to stay and learn storytelling, she would leave.

So I went around the room asking her team how they liked to be communicated to. Did they prefer:

1. facts and stats

2. stories and examples?

As expected, the responses varied between the two options. Some of us are more left-brain aligned with our thinking, so we like lots of data, research and factual information. Others are more right-brain aligned, and like stories and examples that provide meaning to the data. But very rarely do we only rely on just one side. Most of us want a combination of both facts and stories.

I explained that this is the reason, when it comes to communicating, that we need to think less about how *we* like being communicated to and more about how the *audience* prefers to be communicated to. Just because we rely on logic, for example, this does not mean our audience does.

Now, if you have such a variety of communication preferences in a room of 12 people, imagine the variety in an audience of thousands. This is why communicating only in your preferred style is not only inconsiderate, but also ineffective.

After morning tea, everyone returned for the rest of the session, including the reluctant CEO.[1]

If we want to communicate effectively, we can't just focus on our own preferred style of communication; we need to be more balanced.

Just give me the facts

In business, we tend to lean towards focusing on logic and logic alone. We have been taught, perhaps all our career, that being professional is about being data driven and providing just facts and figures. We have probably been told by managers in the past to 'just show me the facts' or 'business is not personal'. You may have even been told not to show any emotion.

[1] Fair to say, I have never worked with this company since ... nor do I want to.

The reality is that as humans we are emotional beings and, while logic has its place in business, most of the time it informs but does not influence or inspire.

Importantly, logic usually does not influence or change behaviour.

It is very well documented how influential emotion is in consumer behaviour. For example, in *Descartes' Error*, Antonio Damasio, a professor of neuroscience at the University of Southern California, shows that when we evaluate brands, we buy based on our personal feelings and experiences, rather than on the more logical information provided, such as product features and benefits.

As far back as 2500 years ago, Aristotle suggested you need three things when you're trying to influence and persuade people:

1. *Logos:* sound logic

2. *Ethos:* personal credibility

3. *Pathos:* emotional connection.

This still rings true today.

Now, I don't think we need any additional help with using logic in our business communications. I think we have that under control with our pie charts and bar graphs and excel spreadsheets. What we do need a bit more convincing in is the power of story.

You need sound logic, personal credibility AND emotional connection to engage your audience.

The magic of story

Stories are one of the most powerful ways to engage your audience because, when done right, they:

- provoke emotions that engage and interest them

- make them feel a connection towards you, as the person telling the story

- help build trust and credibility

- influence them into making a decision

- help them understand and remember messages better, and for longer.

This combination of benefits reminds me of when Lisa Simpson told Homer that bacon, ham and pork chops all came from the same animal and he responded with, 'Yeah right, Lisa. A wonderful "magical" animal'.

Story is truly a wonderful magical beast, and here's why.

Create a connection and increase trust

In chapter 3 I talked about how we are all crying out to be better connected to each other. Well, good stories help us to feel just that.

Neuroeconomist Paul Zak has done some amazing research into the powerful impact the hormone oxytocin has on the brain when we tell stories. Oxytocin is often referred to as the trust hormone and our bodies naturally release it when we are with people we love and trust. Zak's research showed that it is also released when we listen to stories. So, according to Zak's research, this oxytocin that is released when we hear a good story helps us create a connection with the storyteller.

So with the overall decline of trust in business, it is more important than ever to use storytelling to create a real connection with your audience.

Influence your audience to make decisions

As already mentioned, research by neuroscientist Antonio Damasio shows emotion plays a significant role when it comes to people making decisions.

Damasio's research involved examining people with damage to their frontal lobe. This is the area of the brain responsible for forming emotions.

Except for their inability to feel or express emotions, the participants in Damasio's research group had normal intellect in terms of memory, attention span, language comprehension and expression. Critically, though, they were also unable to readily make decisions, such as deciding what to eat.

Damasio showed this indecision came from participants constantly analysing the pros and cons of each decision to a point of no decision. The participants being unable to feel emotions removed the emotional side of the decision. And without this emotional factor, they simply couldn't decide. (If you have ever said, 'I know I should have the salad but I feel like the burger', you have made an emotional decision.)

Another neuroscientist, Christine Comaford, author of the *New York Times* bestseller *Smart Tribes: How Teams Become Brilliant Together*, also states that 90 per cent of human behaviour and decision-making is driven by our emotions.

Not understanding the role emotion plays in decisions can make life extremely frustrating for us as leaders, sales people or even parents. Bestselling author Dale Carnegie put it well when he said, 'When dealing with people, let us remember we are not dealing with creatures of logic. We are dealing with creatures of emotion'.

All the research shows that storytelling is critical when creating an emotional connection with another person.

If you're looking to influence and communicate more effectively, you must balance logic (the facts) with emotion (the stories).

Help your audience understand the message

If you need any more convincing of the magical power of story, let's look at Paul Zak's research on oxytocin and storytelling once more. His research also showed that when we listen to a story with a bit of tension in it, the brain produces the stress hormone cortisol, which helps us to focus.

Zak's research shows that character-driven stories that provoke emotion result in a better understanding of key messages in the story. More importantly, listeners are better able to recall the main points weeks later.

The key here is *character-driven* stories — that is, stories about people, not companies. This is why case studies and business examples do not make very good stories when it comes to creating an emotional connection with your audience, and them remembering your message. Case studies can be a valuable source of information, but they are still logic-based none the less.

Stories influence us in our decision-making process, along with helping us create a connection with the storyteller and increasing our trust in them.

Stories that evoke emotion help us remember messages more effectively than logical information.

Make your story personal

So how do we actually use stories at work?

The simplest way is to think of a personal story from your life and link it to a business context.[2] You could tell a story from when you were a child, or about your children, your friends or your parents.

Take, for example, the following story from Anne Bennett, Executive General Manager of Transformation at NAB. I worked with Anne several years ago when she wanted to share a personal story with her team around integrity and doing the right thing.

This is the story she shared:

> My dad was an elite swimmer when he was young, and at sixteen years old he was in the backstroke finals to make it into the 1964 Tokyo Olympic Games team for Australia.

---

[2] My previous book *Stories for Work* has over 50 examples of how people have shared personal stories in business to great effect.

Dad flew out of the blocks and was out in front of all his competitors, but as he approached his turn at 50 metres, he missed the wall. Knowing he hadn't made the touch, he swam back, touched the wall and kept racing.

Dad came in seventh that day and missed out on making the Olympic squad. After finishing, the judges told him that they hadn't seen the missed touch (it was well before technology recorded this) and if he had kept going, he would have come first and potentially broken a world record.

Dad would always tell my sister and me that he has never regretted that split-moment decision and, even though the judges didn't see the missed touch, he knew he had missed it and he knew turning back was the right thing to do. For me, doing the right thing is a lifelong lesson shown to me by my dad and the integrity he showed that day.

When I think of integrity, I think of my dad. We will often be faced with situations in business where we have to decide if we go back and touch the wall or not. It is at these times I always ask myself what my dad would do.

Anne used the power of analogy in this story. That is, she took the story of what her dad did, and then connected this to what we all can do in the business context. The best stories use these kinds of relatable analogies and metaphors to connect and inspire, and then make a larger point. Anne's story showed her team that integrity is important to her. The obvious realisation to her audience is that this was the way she was raised. Integrity is what her parents expect of her, and it is what she expects of herself and what she expects of the people she leads.

Anne said that after sharing the story, she noticed a change in behaviour from her team. When a decision was due to be made she would often hear one of her team say, 'This is our go back and touch the wall moment', which resulted in not only the right decision being made but also everyone in the team supporting it.

When you share personal stories you will create a more authentic connection with your audience.

Write it out: Stories in written communication

Stories don't always have to be told verbally—in face-to-face meetings, for example, or presentations. They can also be included in written formats.

My next example comes from a real estate agent, and her newsletter no less. When you hear 'newsletter from a real estate agent', I am guessing you're not filled with excitement or anticipation of what it could contain. However, this one is different.

This is a newsletter from Erin Rush, a real estate agent at Harcourts in Wellington, New Zealand, that I was alerted to by a client.

> Good grief my husband is watching *George and Mildred* on the telly. It's so bad it's good. The episode he's watching is where George attempts to sell their house without telling Mildred. There are the expected misunderstandings, double entendres, and the eventual reveal. The great line when Mildred cottons on and asks George if he'd like to be buried or burned. Gold.
>
> It's very clear today—if there is more than one name on the title of a property, it's in a trust or a company—all owners have to sign both the agency agreement and the sale and purchase agreement. Perhaps back then (1976) it would not have been common to have the missus on the title. I must ask my mum and dad.
>
> In 1976 I was six, the youngest of four kids. Mum was 28. She and Dad had gotten busy. I remember her surprise 30th because we got dressed in our church clothes and pretended nothing was happening when she got back from netball practice. Mum said she thought something was up when we were sitting unnaturally still in the lounge and not hitting each other. Then she went into the kitchen and all the friends yelled 'surprise' and there was a huge party, which I don't remember, except for me and my 9-year-old brother getting up in the morning and sneaking the dirty fag-ends out of the ashtrays and having a quick puff, and Mrs O'Malley wearing an orange kaftan remarkably like that worn by Mildred in tonight's episode.
>
> Which brings me nicely to the 70s two bedroom townhouse I have for sale today in Maupuia. A great buy for a first home buyer, retiree,

investor or those looking for a small home. I wonder how many kaftans have graced that home?

Have a wonderful week and do let me know if there's anything you see here you'd like to know more about, and if I can show you through.

Cheers!

Erin

I love how this story leads you in and then includes just a subtle sell at the end. And it's written as if it's being told verbally, using a conversational tone (and even admitting some perhaps questionable childhood decisions). How refreshing, different and real is that?

When I contacted Erin about her newsletter, she told me she'd read other newsletters where there was no connection — 'you might as well be looking at a newspaper ad'. So she focused on finding that connection. As she said, her 'job is actually about people, not houses. And people buy from people they like'. Perfect!

I know from experience that I receive the most feedback and interaction from my audience when I share personal stories in my weekly blogs. I have also heard, time and time again, the same result from others who do the same. (Erin even has people stay on her newsletter list, long after they have bought a house, just for a laugh. Though you can bet who they'll be contacting when they next want to move ...)

Stories can be shared in so many different forms. You can share stories in a one-on-one situation or on stage speaking to 1000 people. You can use them internally with your team, with people you mentor, with your kids and with your clients.

They can also be in a verbal or written format, shared face to face, over teleconference, in videos and in blogs and newsletters.

The real point is to use them!

Both stories and facts have a powerful part to play when it comes to real and authentic communication, so develop a suite of stories you can use, and prepare and practise them. (See chapter 8 for tips on delivering your stories with confidence and impact. Also see my previous book, *Stories for Work*, for help with developing a range of stories for different contexts and purposes.)

Remember, stories are like fish 'n' chips—you can't have one without the other. (Well, you can but obviously it is not as good.)

To create real connection with your team, your peers and your stakeholders, you need to build trust and credibility—fast. Sharing personal stories will help you do just that.

Get REAL now

- Balance your facts and stats with stories and examples.

- Learn how to bring in emotion instead of just logic when trying to communicate in a more engaging way.

- Use stories to build trust, and to influence and persuade others.

- Use stories if you want your message to be better remembered and recalled.

- Share stories verbally and in written format.

CHAPTER 7

VISUALISE INFORMATION

Think of the last time someone was explaining a process to you and you just couldn't quite 'get it'. So perhaps you asked, 'Can you draw it or map it out for me?'

Visuals help us understand and remember messages better.

Dr John Medina, author of *New York Times* bestseller *Brain Rules*, has done extensive research on how visuals aid with memory. He says, 'The more visual the input becomes, the more likely it is to be recognised and recalled'.

In fact, he says that 90 per cent of what the brain processes is visual information. People generally understand and remember pictures, diagrams, models and images better and faster than they do words alone.

Remember the walls of your classroom when you were a kid? They were likely plastered with images showing that 'A is for apple' and 'B is for banana' (with, of course, images of apples and bananas). This increased retention of visual information.

As we moved through our schooling and entered the workplace, however, this all stopped.[1]

Visuals are very much like stories—they are something we have used to help us learn and remember key messages since we were very little. Unfortunately, once we enter a 'serious job' visual representations all seem to be replaced by boring facts and stats, and lots and lots of text and bullet points.

Yet the 2018 State of Attention report presented by Prezi showed that engaging content must have 'a compelling narrative combined with stimulating visuals and dialogue'.

In the report:

- 55 per cent of business professionals say a great story captures their focus and keeps them engaged with content

- 41 per cent of business professionals say stimulating dialogue keeps them interested in content

- 33 per cent report visual stimulation is critical in maintaining their engagement.

The issue is that we usually resort to PowerPoint to help us visualise and present information, yet rarely do we use visuals correctly in our slides.

The problem with PowerPoint

If you have no idea what an overhead projector is[2], it's likely you were born late in the '80s, so let me explain (or you can just do a search on Google Images now). An overhead projector is a big and clunky, kind of milk crate looking thing with a bedside lamp stuck on top, used to project images onto a screen (or wall) back in the day.

[1] And not because you knew the alphabet by then.
[2] You can actually still buy overhead projectors today if you want to go retro.

A clear piece of A4 plastic (a transparency) was used sort of like a slide. You'd type out your content, load a transparency into the printer, race back to your computer to press print, and then have to race back to the printer to grab the transparency before anyone else printed their stuff on it by mistake. (Oh, the joys.)

With the overhead projector as our norm, it is no wonder that the introduction of PowerPoint was met with such excitement. (I can only imagine that this is close to what it would have been like when people replaced horse-drawn carriages with cars or candles with electricity.)

At our fingertips, we had the power to transform any presentation into a piece of gripping entertainment. Remember the 'swooooshhhh' sound when you changed slides? Or the little stick figures you could insert, pointing their finger at something?

With all these fancy features in PowerPoint, there was no possible way our presentations could ever be boring again, right?

How wrong we were. So very wrong.

If PowerPoint was a prescribed drug, it would have been withdrawn from sale and banned years ago for severely impacting our ability to communicate.

Worse yet, most of us are now addicts.

A company called Forethought launched PowerPoint on 20 April 1987. It was only three months later that Microsoft acquired it for $14 million. Which means this product has been around for more than 30 years—so you would think that, by now, we would know how to use it properly. Unfortunately, we don't.

The same goes for all of the alternative options we now have, such as Keynote, SlideShare and Prezi.

It isn't any fault of the software; the communication problem simply comes down to the systemic poor use of the software.

When I run training workshops for companies, I find myself walking past the glass walls of other meeting rooms and viewing text-heavy slides littered with bullet points stared at by audiences with glazed expressions and heavy eyelids. Can the presenter not see what I see or feel the lack of energy in the room?

We are so conditioned to poor slides, however, that we now accept this experience.

The way we currently use PowerPoint slides involves three main problems:

1. a document crammed with information

2. a script for the speaker

3. a tool to hide behind.

Let's look at each.

A document crammed with information

Emma Bannister is a presentation pro and the founder and CEO of Presentation Studio. She has seen a lot of presentations in her time — mostly bad ones. In her book *Visual Thinking: How to Transform the Way you Think, Communicate and Influence with Presentations* she explains why these presentations are so bad:

> Many companies believe that sharing everything and blinding their audience with numbers is the best way to be transparent and open — that couldn't be further from the truth! This will only put the people you are trying to engage off, and make them lose interest faster.
>
> Content-heavy presentations are confusing. There's no point doing all the work on the words and numbers if you overcrowd your visuals with facts and stats and dense text that is barely legible.

Her arguments are backed up by research investigating the way human brains process information. Professor John Sweller is a researcher at the University of New South Wales, Australia. He is well known for his work on cognitive load theory, and his research in this area has shown that the human brain processes information better if it is in either written or verbal format... not both.

To receive information simultaneously—for example, through the PowerPoint slides and the presenter's speech—reduces the brain's ability to process the data because our senses are working overtime. Professor Sweller agrees, stating:

> It is effective to speak to a diagram, because it presents information in a different form. But it is not effective to speak the same words that are written, because it is putting too much load on the mind and decreases your ability to understand what is being presented.

So, expecting your audience to read slides as you are talking reduces the effectiveness of your presentation.

Some of the best presentations don't use any slides at all—for example, Simon Sinek's TEDx talk 'How great leaders inspire action', with over 41.5 million views on YouTube.

It is more important than ever to cut all the crap from your presentation.

A script for the speaker

Using PowerPoint is an easy out for the presenter because they think they don't need to prepare or practise their presentation—they can just read their slides like a speech. (Ironically, I have often witnessed speakers using this approach when talking about end-user design or customer-centred strategy.)

This is just bad form, plain and simple. Is it any wonder your audience are falling asleep in their seats? How can you expect them to be engaged when you're not even making an effort to engage them?

Your slides should always be used as an aid for the audience and not a script for you.

As Bannister goes on to explain:

> Practise your presentation out loud, not just in your head. This will give you an accurate idea of timing. Let your personality and passion shine, give the audience more than a report. Ask your friends, colleagues or family to critique you.
>
> Don't try and memorise the script, word for word—it's near impossible! When I first started trying to give my presentations like this I froze. I would literally stop breathing and the oxygen stopped flowing into my brain so I had no idea where I was in the presentation script or what to say next.

So if you need notes as a speaker, keep them separate from the slides that you present to the audience.

A tool to hide behind

Many years ago, a friend called me to ask for help with his PowerPoint presentation. I advised him that my technical skills were not very good because I hardly ever used PowerPoint. He responded in disbelief, 'But if you don't have slides, everyone will be looking at you!' Exactly.

Everyone is looking at me because, as a speaker, I want the full attention of my audience—that is the point.

People are in the room to listen to your message. If you want them to simply read from the slides, save everyone a whole lot of time by cancelling the presentation and sending them an email instead.

In his *New York Times* bestselling book *TED Talks*, Chris Anderson talks about slides and suggests that 'the first question to ask yourself is whether you actually need any of it'. He goes on to point out that one-third of TED's most viewed talks do not use any slides at all. (And just think of how engaging a TED Talk is.)

My preference is to avoid slides whenever possible and use a whiteboard or a flipchart to illustrate a point. However, when I'm speaking to a large group, it can be difficult for everyone to see this, so out of necessity (to cater for the needs of the audience), I use slides.

> *The trick is to make sure you are using slides for the right reasons—to help your audience, not to hide behind.*

Power your points instead

So now we've got our over-reliance on PowerPoint out of the way, what do we actually do about it? How do we use visuals properly in our presentations, in team meetings and client briefings, or even emails?

Different types of visuals can help you communicate more effectively. These include:

- pictures and photos

- props

- videos

- models, graphs and infographics.

The types of visuals you might use depend on the context you're presenting in. So let's look further at each option.

Pictures and photos

I was once involved in a long-term transformational project and, after two and a half years and the change was complete, I needed to do a series of presentations to the business. The first slide I put up in my presentation was a picture of my daughter, who was nearly two years old at the time. I spent about 30 seconds talking about her, knowing people would be thinking, *Why is she telling us about her daughter?* I then said, 'You are probably wondering why I am talking about my daughter. The reason is that when we started this project, I was six weeks pregnant'. One of my key messages was about how intensive and long this change had been, and I believed that making this point via my daughter's age would have more impact than just saying we have been working on this for two and a half years...and it did.

A picture paints a thousand words, so scrap the actual 1000 words and use a picture instead.

I once worked with a senior leader called Nicole who would often be asked to speak about diversity and inclusion. She regularly began her presentation by sharing a story about the back problems she experienced while growing up. As a result, she wore a brace over her torso for several years. While she shared this story, she simply showed a photo of herself as a girl wearing this brace.

Insert a picture that represents your message and, as often as possible, keep it real by using your own photos or high-quality unusual images. Poor-quality overused stock photos are the clipart of the 21st century!

Indeed, Bannister offers some great tips when it comes to image selection:

> Avoid hand-shaking figures, smiling suited people, little vector people standing on arrows and graphs, and predictable and boring stock images that have been used a hundred times before.

She believes that these kinds of cheesy stock photos can really turn your audience off.

If you must have text to accompany your picture, keep it simple. Remember: less is more.

Props

I worked with a general manager recently at Telstra called Jon Lipton. Jon needed to present to 100 of his team the importance of trusting in a new strategy. He included not only a story as part of his presentation but also a prop—an actual cricketing trophy—that he brought out at the appropriate time to help his message hit home.

This is the story he shared:

> After I had finished high school, a small group of us joined the local cricket club, Koonung Heights, based in the eastern suburbs of Melbourne.

For me this was a great social thing and a good way to stay in touch with some good mates. Every Tuesday and Thursday night we would meet for training. We would get together afterwards for a meal and a few beers—the only downside for me was having to play cricket for six hours every Saturday.

It became apparent to most of my peers reasonably quickly that I had no real ability to play the game. I couldn't bowl and wasn't very good at batting. For those who know the game, if you're not a fantastic batter and you don't bowl you need to be a great fielder.

As a fielder I was great. I'd catch everything that came near me. The only problem was that I could only do this at training; when it came to a match I was completely hopeless. I was so bad I managed to drop a catch every game for an entire season. In fact, this became quite a joke—even to the point where in the cricket season 1992/1993, I won this award for the worst fielder in the entire competition.

Over the next season as a cricket club, we got a bit more serious about winning and went through a bit of change. We hired a coach and we grew our teams from the z division into a number of different grades. Most of my mates started moving into some of the higher grades and most of the social discussions would be centred on events in the higher grades.

I recall one night chatting to the coach. While I can't remember his name, I clearly remember the conversation. 'Keep training hard,' he told me. 'At some point this will translate into the game. *Trust the strategy; trust the process.*'

I continued to catch everything at training, and continued to drop everything in the actual game. Looking back on it now, I had such self-doubt I remember dreading the ball being hit my way as I knew I would drop it. While it almost feels like it was overnight, I'm sure in reality it was over a longer period of time where I went from 'please don't hit it to me', to 'I want the ball hit to me so I can catch it'. Sure enough I went on to win the most ever catches in a season 1994/95.

I'm sharing this with you not to show you my z-grade fielding award of 1993, but rather because every time I feel self-doubt or doubt if we are heading in the right direction I remember my cricket coach's words from some 30 years ago: *'Trust the strategy; trust the process. Trust the strategy; trust the process'.*

I invite you to think about the importance of sticking to a strategy and to trust the process even when things seem tough or there doesn't appear like there is light at the end of the tunnel. Together we may even catch more balls than we drop.

Jon pulled out his actual trophy at the appropriate time in the story and left it on display. The story was already creating a visual but the prop of the trophy really added to this visual effect, making the message more memorable.

Using these kinds of props in presentations can be unexpected and leave a lasting impression on your audience. Props are a memorable way to provide a visual with your message. Just make sure your prop does leave the right visual. Make sure it's appropriate for your audience and is connected to the story. Don't have one just for the sake of having one.

Props don't have to be anything grand or outrageous, as long as they provide an opportunity to get your audience's attention.

In my workshops and presentations on storytelling, I bring in things like toothpaste and postcards that highlight good and not so good uses of stories. Both have a very short story written on them that I read out to the audience. One is good, and one is not so good. When I am talking about a good story I hold up the prop that relates to that story, and when I am talking about the bad use of storytelling I hold up the other one. I use these props as the visual reminder of what makes a good story and what makes a bad story.

Videos

In my experience, good use of video is just like sharing a story: it helps you hone your point in an engaging way.

You may recall videos such as 'Leadership lessons from geese' that became popular in the '90s (if you haven't seen this video, Google the phrase to see a few different options). During leadership programs or conferences, these videos would be used to visualise how, when geese fly together in a V formation, they can fly 70 per cent further than if flying alone — showing that when we work together, we have better performance as a team.

You can also use video to introduce some humour into your presentation. In my workshops, I show one of my Jargon Free Fridays videos to highlight the point that if people used jargon and acronyms in any other aspect of our life besides business, we would call it out for how ridiculous it sounds.

I also show a very funny video of Australian surfer Sabre Norris, who at 11 years old shot to fame when interviewed on morning TV making fun of her dad. Her candid interview shows how real words are easier to visualise and connect with. The interview was so engaging that Sabre ended up being interviewed on *The Ellen DeGeneres Show*. That clip with Ellen has been watch over 55 million times!

Video needs to be used with caution, however. My advice when using video is don't have too many video clips. I remember seeing one presenter speak for about 45 minutes and he included ten videos. It felt like he was using the videos to deflect attention and, therefore, making himself redundant as a speaker.

Just like my advice with a prop, make sure any video you choose is appropriate for your audience and relevant to your message. If it is a video that has gone viral and most people have seen it, make sure you introduce it as such. For example, when I introduce the Sabre Norris video that went viral I always make sure I say something along the lines of, 'This went viral a few years ago so many of you have probably seen it'.

I would also suggest that you should not start or end your presentation with a video. Your voice should be the first and last thing your audience hears. The start of your presentation should focus on your connection with the audience. Conversely, at the end of the presentation, you should be reinforcing your message and potentially your call to action.

Videos can also work well to support your point in an email or newsletter.

Technology makes it very easy these days to insert videos into your communication for greater effect.

Models, graphs and infographics

Again, Simon Sinek's TEDx presentation shows how a simple model of three circles on a whiteboard can really help visualise information and show the relationship between three topics. (His talk is one of the most viewed in history.)

Models like this help people understand what you are talking about.

Of course, graphs that show an abundance of information or detail can be hard to understand, so make sure you highlight the specific things that are relevant to your audience. Remember that, as the presenter, it is your job to determine what is relevant for your audience and ensures their understanding.

If your graph is very detailed and, therefore, hard for people to see, either use the zoom function to focus on a specific point (if you are using presentation software) or have a handout that people in the audience can actually read.

Infographics are becoming increasingly popular as a way to visualise information. The drawback with infographics is that you need special software to produce them and some time and know-how to do it. They can also become too complicated, making it hard for audiences to grasp the main points. While using an infographic may be warranted in some situations, in others simply drawing a few circles on a whiteboard may be all that is required.

You can use a variety of methods to present your information in a more visual way.

Whatever you choose, just make sure you are using visuals to enhance the communication for your intended audience.

Get REAL now

- Ask yourself: Do I really need this PowerPoint presentation?

- Even if you decide you do need slides, reduce the amount of text and number of bullet points on each.

- Consider including personal photos or high-quality images in your communications (not overused stock photos).

- Figure out how you could use props as a visual tool.

- Use videos if they can reinforce a message.

- Draw a simple model on a whiteboard to help with understanding.

- Make sure you simplify graphs so they don't look too overwhelming.

- Try infographics with some help from the right person or software.

CHAPTER 8

DELIVER YOUR CONTENT WITH IMPACT

So by this stage you probably feel like you have done a lot of work. You have put your audience first and figured out how you can communicate more concisely. You have considered how you can communicate logic and facts as well as emotion and stories to ensure you create a greater connection with your audience. You have thought about how you can use visuals to make your communication more impactful and you are ready to stand and deliver.

So what's left?

To be a truly authentic leader and engaging communicator, we need to go against all the prescriptions we've been taught and bring our unique personality into the way we deliver our message.

I truly believe that to communicate in a real and authentic way, it's important to just be YOU.

Can you recall Professor Robert Kelly being interviewed live in 2017 by BBC, and his two children wandering into the room? And remember his wife crawling along the floor in an attempt to stay out of shot as she got them out? He thought he had completely blown the interview and would never be invited back. Yet the result was the complete opposite. People really connected to it because they just saw a real dad doing his job.

Some of the very best authentic speakers I see are prepared to bring their real self to their presentations to connect and engage their audience.

My friend and inspirational speaker Dan Gregory, for example, is a funny and witty man. He shared a story with me about a time he was presenting when the constant sound of a leaf blower was coming from the street below. The noise was distracting not only him, but also his audience.

Being the consummate professional, Dan soldiered on. When the leaf blower finally stopped, he said you could see the physical relief from those in the audience. As the leaf blower began again about five minutes later, there was an audible audience sigh. In response, Dan went over to the window, opened it and yelled out, 'Mate! Buy a bloody broom!' Classic Dan! Dan said he received his biggest laugh for the entire year.

So what stops us from being our real self when it comes to communicating our messages and, in particular, speaking in public? FEAR!

Fear and loathing in public speaking

Hands up if you've ever thought one of the following when thinking about public speaking:

- 'What if no-one laughs at my jokes?'

- 'What if I forget what I am going to say?'

- 'What if no-one asks any questions?'

- 'What if I fall off stage?'

- 'What if I get really nervous? (Oh, too late I am already really nervous.)'

When we allow these thoughts to have a voice, we enter a mindset of 'just get this over and done with'. This is not a good place to be for you or your audience.

Many people fear public speaking and this fear is amplified when the crowd gets larger. Throw a physical stage into the mix and people really start to panic. The bigger the stage, the bigger the audience, the bigger the consequences — and so the bigger the pressure people place on themselves and the bigger the anxiety they feel.

Thinking and verbalising 'I hate public speaking' is a downward spiral and self-fulfilling prophecy.

If you have spoken before in public and got nervous beforehand, you usually assume that you hate public speaking. The next time you speak, you get nervous again and then start to panic that you are getting nervous, so you get even more nervous... and on and on the cycle continues.

You no doubt know that this is your flight or fight response kicking in. This response is our brain's way of saving us from the sabre-toothed tiger, when it was around. As soon as we feel threatened, our body releases a surge of the stress hormones, adrenaline and cortisol (which, in the case of the sabre-toothed tiger, helped us fight it or run away from it).

A certain level of these stress hormones can be advantageous even in public speaking, because they can bring energy as we are about to present. Too much stress and adrenaline, however, can dry up the throat and mouth, increase our heart rate, make us sweat and flush our skin pink. It can also result in our muscles twitching, which is the shaking that people often associate with nerves.

While we can't completely eliminate the release of these stress hormones, nor would we want to, there are ways to reduce the amount released and their effects.

So let's look at a few things you can do that will help you control your nerves, relax and just be yourself while speaking.

Breathe

Yes, breathing might seem obvious, but it is amazing how many people simply stop breathing when they panic, and then breathe shallowly and too quickly.

It's a fact that deep breathing can really help with nerves. It physically sends a message to your brain to calm down and relax.

Various different methods outline how to breathe more deeply, how many seconds you should inhale, hold and exhale for, and how often you should do it. Your best bet is to keep it simple. For example, I find an easy method to remember is to breathe in for four seconds, hold for four seconds and exhale for four seconds, and then repeat four times.

Not really connected to breathing, but also make sure you have some water on hand to soothe a dry throat. Just don't scull big glasses! You probably don't want to desperately need a toilet moments before you present.

Get physical

Like breathing, getting physical before a presentation can really get rid of those annoying stress hormones.

I was once presenting to 200 peers and a handful of clients and speaking agents. As we waited for people to file into the auditorium, someone pumped up the music and Justin Timberlake's 'Can't stop the feeling' blared out. So there I was at the side of the room, waiting for the audience, dancing to the song. (I defy anyone to hear that song and not dance.)

Getting really physical by doing something like dancing can reduce the stress hormones quickly, but you don't need to dance to get physical.

I was presenting to 1000 people in Washington DC. It was in the International Ballroom at the Hilton hotel—where they hold the annual White House Correspondence Dinner that the President usually attends. It was a pretty big deal for me.

A few minutes before I took the stage one of the other presenters gave me a pair of Spider-Man socks. I felt compelled to change into them there and then. With me about to take the stage, I quickly took off my shoes and replaced my plain old black socks with my new pair of Spider-Man ones. Before I knew it, the conference had started and I was on stage. Even that small amount of physical activity helped reduce the stress hormones for me.

So find a way to get physical, even if it's just a little bit physical.

Visualise a positive outcome

Physiologist Edmund Jacobson's research into professional athletes showed that when they visualised specific activities, the muscles in their bodies subtly moved like they were actually performing that movement. The research showed that a person who consistently visualised a certain physical skill develops 'muscle memory', which assisted in boosting performance.

Similar research undertaken by Australian psychologist Alan Richardson also supported Jacobson's findings.

Richardson split basketball players into three random groups. On the first day, all three groups practised free throws for 20 minutes to determine their accuracy. Over the next 20 days, the three groups were instructed to undertake different activities. The first group practised free throws every day for 20 minutes. The second group did nothing. The final group spent 20 minutes visualising, but not practising free throws.

On the 20th day each group spent 20 minutes practising free throws and Richardson measured the percentage of improvement. The first group, who had practised daily, improved by 24 per cent. The second group, who had done nothing, showed no improvement at all. The third group, who had only spent 20 minutes visualising, did 23 per cent better. So the players who had only visualised were still able to perform almost as well as the group who physically practised.

Richardson also found the most effective visualisation occurred when the person visualising feels and sees what they are doing.

Visualising success works because the brain cannot distinguish between reality and imagination. After you have visualised something in detail, when you actually encounter the real situation your mind feels like it has done the action before.

Visualising successful public speaking helps improve your communication and presentation skills.

When I have a significant presentation to deliver, I start visualising this presentation days before. I visualise what I am wearing, walking on stage and seeing the audience laugh at my first joke. I imagine how that will feel, especially when I get a round of applause.

Visualisation isn't only for big presentations, either. If you have a significant client meeting or team meeting, or even a difficult one on one or perhaps job interview, it could well be worth giving visualisation a go.

Do something different

A senior executive leader I was working with was tasked with introducing the conference session after lunch. The conference took place in a large room, with approximately 250 people sitting at tables of ten.

Instead of taking to the stage, he decided to start talking from the very back of the room. By wearing a lapel microphone, he was clearly audible but not visible, so everyone was looking around to see where he was. It only took a few seconds for them to find him. He then slowly made his way to the front by meandering past most of the tables, finishing his speech once he was on stage. This leader created a big impact by doing something just a little bit different in combination with sharing a personal story.

You can still be professional and show off your personality by doing something unusual or unexpected.

I use a similar approach when I do my storytelling presentations. At one point, I want to take my audience through what makes a story and what the important considerations are when implementing storytelling in business. Instead of just listing my content, I get the audience to discuss it. Normally my audiences are seated around tables, so they can easily interact. After a few minutes, I make my way off stage and start sharing their ideas from the back of the room. This allows me to interact with the audience on a more personal level.

The size and layout of the room will determine how I do this. If I am presenting in front of thousands of people, I don't use this approach. Likewise, if I am in an auditorium or lecture-style set up, this also doesn't work. Wherever possible, however, I request for the participants to be seated around tables. And even while walking around the audience may not always be possible, asking people to discuss an idea, even in pairs in an auditorium, still works.

Never be constrained by the expectations of how you think a presentation should be. Be you!

Another way to take control and break free with your presentation could be to have someone interview you instead of you making a traditional speech. This allows a more casual approach and lends itself to integrating more stories to illustrate your messages.

I recall working with one CEO on his presentation and the personal stories he shared clearly demonstrated his values. When I suggested we do an interview instead of a presentation, his relief was visible. He knew what questions I was going to ask and the corresponding messages he wanted to communicate, but he also gave me the freedom to ask additional questions. This format allowed him to demonstrate his real self.

Choose clothes for confidence

In her book *Daring Greatly*, Brené Brown shares a story from when she was speaking at one of the largest leadership events in the world in Chicago. The event organisers had strongly recommended that she wear business attire, which she did. Brown then describes sitting with another speaker, 'staring down at my black slacks and pumps and feeling like an imposter. Or like I was going to a funeral'. She confessed to the other speaker that she felt like she was playing 'dress-ups'. The other speaker told her she 'looked nice' but Brown knew her face was saying, 'I know. It's hard. But what can we do?'

With that, Brown couldn't take it any longer and grabbed her suitcase, went to the bathroom and changed into her jeans, navy shirt and clogs — something she felt confident in and, more important to her, authentic in.

And feeling authentic is important when your message, like Brown's, is on authenticity and courage. On seeing her outfit change, the other speaker said, 'Awesome. You're brave'.

What you are wearing can have a significant impact on your confidence. When dressing for a presentation or an important meeting, make sure you wear clothes that YOU feel confident in. (The YOU is in capitals here because you don't want to be persuaded by what other people tell you looks good or what you need to wear to feel confident or look 'professional'.)

If you don't feel confident in it, then don't wear it.

My one slight little rule with what you wear when presenting is to be slightly above the dress code of your audience or at least be different. I often wear good brogue shoes that are very different from what my audience might be in—for example, they might be shiny silver or glittery. They become something that sparks a conversation and makes me stand out.

Just find something that you feel authentic and confident in, because this will affect your confidence when you communicate.

Stop hiding

Real communication is all about engagement and connection. Unfortunately, due to nervousness or lack of confidence, too many of us try to hide behind our notes.

Reading our notes instantly creates a disconnect with the audience. Regardless if you are communicating in a meeting or on stage, try to avoid reading your notes. No-one knows what your notes contain, and if you forget something the only person who ever knows is you. And even if the audience did know, they don't care.

Have the courage to ditch the notes.

People often resort to the safety of the lectern while reading their notes. This means you not only are reading but also now have a physical barrier between you and your audience. This is disastrous if you are short because all people can see is a head popping over the top!

Wherever possible request a lapel microphone, which gives you freedom to walk among your audience and helps create a stronger connection. You can also still walk back to the lectern or desk if you need to refer to your notes.

Above all else, have the courage to stand and deliver—whether it's face to face, over the phone or in a room full of peers.

Involve everyone

Have you ever been in a meeting when someone brings in a printed PowerPoint presentation and then proceeds to flip through the pages?

When this happens, I do two things:

1. I try to ascertain how many pages are in the pack to prepare myself for death by PowerPoint.

2. I disengage because I assume the person has come to present rather than converse, and they are going to get through all of their slides and dot points, regardless of anything else.

Real and authentic communication is not about blurting out a bunch of information at people, but respecting and facilitating others' input.

If you want a more engaging and conversational style instead of one-way presentations, you should consider involving your audience by asking questions.

As a speaker, understand that it can be intimidating to ask questions, especially if part of a large audience. Most people don't like public speaking and some people assume that their question or comment is not valid so they are reluctant to ask it in fear of looking silly. I have lived through the experience of the dreaded silence after asking for questions from the audience, but you can use certain techniques to encourage participation.

I tend to sit out the first few seconds of silence by taking a few sips of water. In reality this is about 10 seconds, but to others in the audience it feels much longer. Then I make a joke that I am being paid by the minute so I'm happy to wait it out. That always results in people laughing and someone always ends up asking a question. Everyone hates that awkward silence, including your audience, so it is only a matter of time before someone 'feels sorry' for you and rescues you.

You can, and should, do certain things to gather input from your audience—don't just assume they have nothing to say.

When I speak at conferences, I also always factor in time to be present at the break afterwards. Without exception, I will always have people come up to me during this time to ask a question they were reluctant to ask in the public forum.

You could also give the audience a minute to discuss the presentation—either at their tables, if that is the seating arrangement, or with the person next to them. After this, you can ask for questions or comments based on what they discussed. This generates that 'safety in numbers' feeling and also usually generates better quality input.

What about the f-bomb?

I recall the first time I dropped the f-bomb on stage at a conference in New Zealand. (I thought Australians were the biggest swearers in the world until I started to spend some time in New Zealand.)

It was a relatively small audience of about 80 people and my session was quite interactive. At the end, a gentleman stood up and said, 'I agree with what you are saying because yesterday we had someone talking about strategic brand narrative and I was thinking to myself, *I don't even know what the fuck that means*'. I responded with, 'You are right. What does that fucking mean?' To which I almost got a standing ovation and I wrapped up my session.

Straight afterwards a woman approached me, explaining she was the HR manager. My heart stopped and my head was saying, 'Fuck, fuck, fuck, I am in so much trouble for dropping the f-bomb'. But instead she said, 'That was fucking awesome'.

I know when I swear on stage, the vast majority of people respond to it positively. If they didn't, I wouldn't do it.

To swear or not to swear should be determined by whether it is appropriate to your audience and if you are comfortable with it.

I know people will adamantly disagree with me and suggest it is never appropriate to swear in a business context, and especially on stage. I understand this argument, but I believe it is okay if it's appropriate to your audience and it does not damage your brand.

Take Gordon Ramsay, for example, who has built an empire and several TV shows on the back of his foul language (and, yes, of course his cooking).

If you don't normally swear and you think your audience would be offended by coarse language, don't swear. That's a no-brainer. If, however, you are like me and you don't mind a bit of coarse language, and you don't think your audience will be offended, it's probably okay.

Above all else, if in doubt, leave it out.

Mastery matters

At the end of the day, getting better at how you communicate involves practice. With time, you will get more confidence, and with confidence you will get better at communicating.

However, you can do some extra things to help facilitate this journey, especially if public speaking is involved.

Learn from the pros

In 2018 I went to see Jerry Seinfeld on stage when he visited Australia. He was speaking at a large arena with thousands of people in the audience. Before he came out, the stage was set with only a bar stool and a bottle of water—that's it. As the audience waited for him to take the stage and excitement built, so did my curiosity about how he was going to use this large and predominately empty stage. And use it he did.

During the presentation, Seinfeld would stomp across the stage to illustrate a point. He would walk right to the front of the stage raising his voice and throwing his arms up and out in exaggerated movements to show his anger at something. It was funny, engaging and effective.

After the event I decided that maybe I could be a bit like Seinfeld. So at my next large keynote presentation in Singapore, I decided an exaggerated 'Seinfeld like' action would be warranted at a certain point in my presentation — and hopefully funny, engaging and effective.

When I reached that point, I walked to the front of the stage and yelled out, 'This is not a story' while in an exaggerated move I flung a postcard I was talking about in the air. As it spun across the heads of the audience, I threw my hands up in disgust.

Besides the one woman who nearly got hit in the forehead by the postcard spinning through the air, the other 499 people in the audience burst out laughing...and it felt good.

I am not suggesting for a second you should just copy other people, but you can start to observe the masters and, if you like what you see and you think it would work for your audience, you can then give it a try.

Just because you observe that it works for one person does not mean you have to adopt it. The action still needs to be authentic to you and appropriate for your audience.

If mastery matters to you, I encourage you to observe people who do presentations well. That could be someone you work with or a TED presenter or someone at the next conference you go to. Take note of what the very good speakers are doing or not doing. Then experiment with some things to see if they work for you and help you become a better communicator.

Own your genius

Natasha Pincus created and directed the music video clip of Gotye's 'Somebody that I used to know'. This video is one of the most viewed clips in history and has won multiple awards around the world. After the success of the video, many people claimed Natasha was a 'genius'. It got her thinking about this — to the point that she wrote a book titled *I Am Not a GENIUS and So Are You*.

In the book she writes that the act of believing you are a genius makes you more creative, more empathetic and more productive. You dare more, believe more and commit more when you believe you're a genius. She says, 'it means accepting that Genius is a label that can't be given to you by anyone but yourself' ... but only 'when you get out of your own way'.

I communicate the same message when I conduct my two-day Thought Leadership Intensive program, which is designed to help clever people develop their ideas to increase their influence and profile in their own company and industry. The process involves them getting clarity on their own genius (what they are good at and what they want to be known for) and then teaching them a process to deepen their thinking and develop their ideas more thoroughly than they have done in the past. This brings real thoroughness and elegance to their ideas so they have the confidence to speak and write about their area of expertise on a more regular basis. Doing so not only informs and educates the people around them but also increases their influence both internally to their company and externally to their industry.

It is worth spending time developing your ideas and concepts so you can spread them to your people in both the written and spoken formats.

Reflect and refresh

When I run training workshops or do keynotes, I always rely on a couple of key stories but, depending on the client's needs or the audience, I will also share new and updated stories.

You need to evolve your communications to make sure they are relevant and fresh.

Reflecting on your communication style on a regular basis is also a good practice to get into. The analysis doesn't have to be time consuming and it doesn't have to happen after each communication. Instead, when you do it, it can simply be a quick evaluation of what worked and what didn't.

Some questions to ask yourself are:

- What really worked and should I do more of it?

- What didn't work that I would not do again?

- What sort of worked that I would do differently next time?

Also reflect on 'How real did this feel?' This applies to any form of communication, such as a team meeting, a sales pitch or even an article or blog you have written.

For example, if you just presented on stage and it felt great or you just wrote an article that seemed to flow easily, think about why that worked for you. This way your future presentations or blogs will feel more real, you will come across as more authentic and you and your audience will enjoy what you produce more.

In addition to self-reflection, seeking out feedback from others can also be beneficial. You could ask a trusted adviser in the audience how it went. Were people engaged?

I know of some presenters who often record their presentations so they can watch or listen to them afterwards and critique them. This can help identify what worked and what didn't.

You may not change anything because of this information, but awareness is the critical first part of moving towards mastery.

Mind the gap: Replacing filler words

I have an unconscious habit of putting my hands in my pocket on stage. Not my whole hand like I am freezing cold, just the fingers. I had a speaking coach who suggested I try to limit the number of times I did this because it was distracting for my audience. It was hard, very hard, to change, and in the end I resorted to wearing pants that did not have pockets.

Another unconscious habit that most people have is using filler words such as 'um', 'you know', 'ah' or 'right?' Or if you are teenager, 'like'. Once your audience notices these filler words, they can become a distraction.

> *The key is to be aware of what your filler words are and then try to reduce them.*

This is also applicable to the written format. Certain words can decrease the impact of your message. For example, I have a tendency to include the word 'just' a lot in my writing—for example, 'I am just sending you an email to just see if you received the invoice we sent'. Or 'I was just wondering when we could expect payment. Just let me know if there is a problem'.

Removing filler words is easier in the written format but much harder when speaking. Here are a few ways to reduce your filler words when presenting.

- Slow down your speaking.

- Replace filler words with a pause. Most people don't like pauses but they can be a powerful way to reduce filler words. Don't be afraid of silence.

- Rehearse your content. If you are confident in what you are saying and that you will remember what you are saying, you will use fewer filler words.

- Identify a variety of other words that you can substitute your one filler word with so it is not repetitive and therefore distracting to your audience. Although trying to reduce them completely is a better strategy.

> *Most leadership positions and positions of influence require you to be really good at communicating.*

So if it is important, I encourage you to keep working on your craft. Invest in this kind of professional development. Find a mentor to help you develop your content, your style and your confidence. Leaders have coaches for all sorts of things and it's worthwhile considering a mentor to help with your presenting.

Read books on the subject. I highly recommend *TED Talks: The Official TED Guide to Public Speaking* by Chris Anderson. The book offers some excellent techniques and advice on how to present on stage and some great stories about maintaining your authentic style.

Regardless of where you are at on this journey, know that communicating in a more engaging way requires that you be prepared to communicate in a more authentic way. You need to be yourself—unless, of course, you are a complete dick. Or as actor and TED Talker Salman Khan said,

> Be yourself [...] If you are generally goofy, then be goofy. If you are emotional, then be emotional. The one exception to that is if you are arrogant and self-centred. Then you should definitely pretend to be someone else.

Get REAL now

- Be prepared to show some personality when you are communicating. Just because someone has scripted something for you doesn't mean you can't change it to your style.

- Know that anxiety around public speaking is normal, so learn what works for you to reduce it.

- Visualise positive outcomes if you are anticipating feeling nervous.

- Be prepared do to something different, regardless of the communication opportunity.

- Wear clothes that you feel confident in when you are presenting.

- Stop hiding behind the lectern and get up closer to the audience.

- Involve your audience with questions.

- Remember—mastery comes with practice. So keep practising!

PART III

How we practise Authentic Leadership

Someone recently asked me what I thought about someone I had worked with for several years. My response was, 'The jury is still out'. Although this person said all the right things, I was not 100 per cent convinced their actions matched their words. The person who had asked for my opinion responded, 'The fact that you are undecided about his authenticity after knowing him for years probably gives you the answer'.

Authentic leadership is hard to define, but easy to sense. No matter what your logic says, whether someone is authentic is almost a gut reaction.

As part of my Authentic Leadership podcast series, I ask leaders what authentic leadership means to them, and the responses vary from being true to yourself and having the courage to take a stand on things, to being consistent with how you are at work and home and just being genuine.

However, I believe authentic leaders display four common traits. They:

1. *Use real words:* They don't hide behind corporate jargon and acronyms because they know this isolates and disengages people, and often leads to miscommunication. They are clear about what they want to say, and communicate this in a way that is easily understood so people can understand and engage with it.

2. *Deal with what's real:* Authentic leaders are prepared to admit their mistakes and say sorry. This is not a half apology along the lines of, 'I am sorry if what I said caused offence' but rather, 'I am sorry for being offensive'. Leaders who deal with what's real show a huge amount of courage.

3. *Show what's real to them:* They are aware of what is important to them and they are prepared to bring that to their leadership role. Congruence exists between their professional and personal values and, in some cases, they are prepared to take a public stand for what they believe.

4. *Know what's real for others:* Authentic leaders are good listeners who take time to find out what is happening with the people they lead and the customers they serve. They have a genuine focus on understanding their people and building a genuine connection.

To really put this into perspective, and practice, we're going to explore these four key traits in detail in this part. The following chapters are packed with case studies and stories of people stepping into authentic leadership ... or, in some cases, not.

CHAPTER 9

USE REAL WORDS

In 2014, Richard Branson wrote a LinkedIn article titled 'Why you should do away with jargon'. His opening paragraph read,

> Some people love speaking in jargon, using fancy words and turning everything into acronyms. Personally, I find this simply slows things down, confuses people and causes them to lose interest. It's far better to use a simple term and commonplace words that everyone will understand, rather than showing off and annoying your audience.

In the article he relayed his experience of not understanding financial jargon for years. He explained that his son's production company was producing a collection of short videos to explain finance in an uncomplicated way — how cool is that?! (And how well-needed.)

You don't have to look far to find examples of everyday people making a conscious effort to use real words and rid the world of bad communication.

As George Orwell included in his six rules for writing English, 'Never use a foreign phrase, a scientific word or a jargon word if you can think of an everyday English equivalent'.

When a biscuit is not a biscuit

Kate Hughes is Chief Audit and Risk Officer at Royal Melbourne Institute of Technology (more commonly known throughout Australia as the acronym RMIT.)

Kate had spent the vast majority of her career in the corporate sector, before moving to one of Australia's largest universities.

The problem was that when Kate first started this new role in a different industry, she was confronted with an overwhelming number of new words, phrases and acronyms. Within just a few days of starting, she had to look up what 'pedagogy' meant and when people referred to a 'Monte Carlo simulation' she thought they were talking about a biscuit.[1]

Kate found herself in every meeting and conversation with her team asking them to explain what most of the terms they were using meant. Many times, what she thought was one thing ended up being something else entirely.

Kate recalls early on in her role reading a ten-page report where the final page was devoted to a glossary that listed all the acronyms used in the previous nine pages. Kate constantly had to refer to the glossary to interpret the information in the report. She found the whole experience not only frustrating but also time consuming.

So she asked her team to rewrite the report with all acronyms expanded and to remove the glossary page that was no longer needed. Guess how long that made the report? The same, ten pages!

Rather than seeing this as a setback, Kate saw this as an opportunity saying, 'The beauty of starting in a new job with no history is you can out all the stupid acronyms'.

Kate has now implemented a communication guideline in her team and that is to expand all acronyms. (I'm sure George Orwell would be so proud of that.)

---

[1] It's a mathematical simulation to calculate risk. Invented in the late 1940s, the creators apparently needed a secret code name for it so named it after the Monte Carlo Casino where one of the creator's uncles would borrow money from relatives to gamble. See how these terms start?!

Of course, exceptions exist to this guideline—for example, if the acronym is commonly used and understood, such as the name of their university (RMIT), it is acceptable. However, an acronym like VAR (value at risk) is not and needs to be expanded every time. This applies not only when speaking but also in the written format.

Kate now has a simple philosophy when it comes to writing papers or emails or any written document. She asks herself three questions:

- Could someone from outside my department read it easily?

- Would they be able to understand it?

- Would they be able to respond to it?

Kate believes that writing with no regard to your audience is 'lazy and poor form' and always inefficient.

When it comes to real communication, Kate sees this as an obligation as a leader, stating, 'If you can't read and understand what I have written, I have failed you'.

Real passion

Kavita Mistry is Head of Technology at ANZ bank. She has a similar insight about real communication and authentic leadership after hearing politician after politician speak. She realised how disengaging it was to hear someone use jargon and attempt to communicate without actually sharing anything insightful or useful. Just as the research I discussed in chapter 3 suggested, Kavita felt a level of distrust when this type of jargon use occurred. She also believes jargon used in this way creates confusion about what the speakers' values are or what they stand for.

As this realisation grew, being genuine and keeping it real is something that Kavita became passionate about.

In the past few years, she has focused on her leadership style, and she says this has evolved from 'focusing on creating harmony within the team to treating individuals as adults and saying it like it is'.

She realised that her focus on harmony when leading was driven by a need to please others, and meant that using jargon or corporate language to shy away from delivering the real message was easier than telling people what was really going on.

For example, using phrases such as 'leverage synergy and drive cross-geographic collaboration' when the real message was about accepting that keeping costs down can result in a workforce that doesn't feel unified and so needing to make the best of the situation and keep our biases in check. Delivering the real message — telling it like it is — also means treating individuals with respect, recognising and addressing our personal biases (and jargon abuses), and challenging others when they don't exhibit the right behaviours.

Kavita has seen the benefits in the shift in her communication style. She says it has resulted in creating a greater level of trust across the team, and an atmosphere where they feel supported when they speak up. This leadership environment has improved the team's ability to change and adapt.

On a personal level, Kavita's changes have led to greater personal confidence, and provided a sense of relief that she can be true to her values and be authentic rather than spending effort on re-engineering the message.

Her approach also means that she challenges herself to go beyond the transactional thoughts and discussions to have more meaningful conversations with colleagues and clients. Opening herself up, and being more real, means others are more likely to do the same.

This is what creates a deeper connection and relationship with the people in her team.

And a bonus tip — getting your team involved in the jargonfreefridays.com challenge is a fun way to raise awareness to the jargon problem and move towards real conversations.

Never forget to make them feel

I first met Stephen Purcell in 2014 when he was CEO and Managing Partner at PPB Advisory. I was doing some business storytelling training with the senior leaders of the firm and Stephen wanted to meet me.

I still remember that meeting at the Laurent Bakery on William Street, in Melbourne. I can't remember much of what we talked about—although I remember he asked me about my kids and he talked about his—but I can still recall how I felt after meeting him. I felt within that short time I had a real connection with him.

While researching for this book I had several people remind me of how Stephen is a leader who always uses real words. When I spoke to Stephen about this, he said something that took me back to our first meeting all those years ago. Mirroring a quote from Maya Angelou, he said that 'when I hear people talk, I often forget what they say but I never forget how I feel'.

He recalls being a kid and listening to adults talk, and experiencing frustration and exclusion when he could not understand what they were talking about. Just as children are no longer excluded from 'adult' conversations, Stephen believes that it is no different as a leader, arguing that, 'As a leader, you need to connect and engage with your staff and when we use jargon we are disconnecting with people not connecting with them'.

Throughout his career, when Stephen has had to address his employees, his main aim is that they walk away from the presentation feeling connected and engaged. He focuses on the outcome of them feeling connected and included. He knows from experience that when people present using jargon he starts to disconnect and he never wants to be that person.

Stephen believes when it comes to communicating, you need to 'avoid jargon, use real words and be yourself'.

Their frame of understanding, not yours

Denise Collazo is Chief of Staff for Faith in Action, based in Florida. I first met Denise at Harvard in 2016 and then again when she attended my Thought Leadership and Business Storytelling training in New York the following year.

Like any business in a specialised industry, Faith in Action have some specific terms related specifically to their industry and organisation. Denise has noticed, however, that when these terms are used with people who are not part of her organisation, this creates unnecessary confusion and tends to distance the person speaking from their listener. Usually, of course, the point of communication is to draw yourself and your institution closer to the listener.

Denise provided a couple of examples for this book to illustrate this point. Her organisation uses the word 'leader' when they are describing the community-based group of volunteer women, men and young people who mobilise and organise others at the community level. This word emerged in response to the community members being described as 'volunteers'—which they felt didn't capture everything this group did for the organisation. Therefore, internally within the organisation, they adopted the word 'leader' for their grassroots community members as a sign of respect for them. As Denise noted, 'Essentially, we wanted to acknowledge they are more than a volunteer; they are a leader'.

The confusion arises when this wording is used outside the organisation—because most people assume when you say 'leader' you are referring to someone in a named or paid position of authority and leadership. 'So, when we talk about our volunteer 'leaders', it often creates confusion for people outside our organisation or people who are new to our organisation. They think we're talking about people like our Executive Director.'

'Federation' is another word they use internally that causes confusion. Faith in Action is a national organisation that consists of state and local federations. Denise said they initially chose the word 'federation' to distinguish their organisation from 'affiliates', which many other organisations, such as the American Red Cross, use. However, when they talk about their member federations people ask, 'Are those your affiliates?' The answer is always, 'Basically, yes'. So, why not simply call them affiliates?

Denise also provided another example of acronyms causing confusion. Their grassroots community members meet regularly in their own congregations or communities and their meetings are called local organising committees, reduced to the acronym LOCs (pronounced 'El-Oh-Cees').

On many occasions, Denise has heard staff speak with funding partners or other external partners and say something like, 'We've been hearing a lot of concerns about specific community issues in our LOCs'. This usually leads to the other person immediately asking, 'What's an LOC?' Denise believes they need to be simply referred to as 'community meetings' to eliminate the need for that clarifying step.

Even the name of their organisation used to be an acronym. They were called PICO National Network, short for People Improving Communities through Organizing. Denise said that whenever she explained the name, people would nod politely and give her a moderately blank stare. So in 2018 they changed their name to Faith in Action. Denise believes the name tells people much more quickly that the organisation is all about people of faith taking action on important issues. The trick now is not to be tempted to reduce that name to FIA.

Denise reflected that the one thing she is learning about jargon is that, 'It is often developed as insider language and, in our case, is all about distinguishing ourselves from our competitors. But when it comes to effective and authentic communication, it's actually most effective to relate yourself to a frame that is already active in the listener's mind'. What a GENIUS insight.

Denise's examples highlight perhaps the real danger in using jargon and acronyms over real words.

The moment we start using jargon with people outside our company or industry is the moment we start to disengage and alienate our audience.

We deliberately use different terms to differentiate ourselves from our competitors. When we do this, however, we are not communicating in a frame that is already active in the listener's mind, which makes it harder to communicate.

When jargon works

I often have people defend the use of jargon, saying that it is more efficient and becomes a shared language. As we have discussed, that is only true when everyone understands that shared language and has a common understanding of what each term and acronym means.

However, it's important to share an example of jargon that works really well.

Mekong Capital is a Vietnam-based firm that invests in struggling companies to help make them profitable. Chris Freund is the firm's founder and partner and I have been working with Chris and the team since March 2018.

What struck me immediately were their unique company values — seven of the eight values are made-up words. They are:

1. *Resultership:* The combination of 'results' and 'leadership', which means holding themselves and others accountable to do whatever is necessary to produce results, but always in a way that is consistent with the other core values.

2. *Springthrough:* The combination of 'spring' and 'through', which is about inspiring themselves and others to step out of comfort zones, play a bigger game and choose empowering contexts, which lead to new actions and breakthrough results.

3. *Victorance:* The combination of 'victory' and 'perseverance', which means a fearless and relentless perseverance until the goal is achieved, regardless of whatever obstacles seem to be in the way.

4. *Beautegrity:* The combination of 'beauty' and 'integrity', which is about honouring their word so that everything works. It also means working together as a unified and powerful force.

5. *Communiplete:* The combination of 'communicate' and 'complete', which means communicating in a direct way so that nothing is misunderstood or unhandled.

6. *Inquisity:* The combination of 'inquisitive' and 'curiosity', which means to relentlessly pursue the root cause and key drivers behind events or trends, and pushing the boundaries in generating game-changing insights.

7. *Jeromosity:* The combination of 'generosity' and the name 'Jerome', who was Chris's mentor, which means to empower others.

8. *Genesis:* This is not a made-up word, and relates to the actions they take, the impact they have and how the world materialises around them. For Mekong Capital, this word means being the cause rather than the effect.

Chris shared with me that the creation of this jargon that they use internally was a very deliberate strategy in creating a shared language. And this shared language goes beyond the made-up names of their company values to other terms they use internally that have a unique meaning to them such as 'breakdown' and 'enrolment'.

What I noticed while working with this company was that not only do all employees fully understand what the values mean but they also refer to them in everyday language. They even call each other out when the value is being displayed or not.

Chris believes that this shared unique language 'totally works for us as it speeds things up and it is very clear when we are talking with each other'. He also adds that when they use these terms with people outside the company, it can be 'confusing' and usually 'shuts things down'. He and the team are, therefore, extremely disciplined in ensuring they do not use these internal terms with outsiders unless they explain them.

Get REAL now

- Expand all acronyms unless they are absolutely common knowledge to everyone.

- Have the courage to ask when you don't know what something means.

- Review all your communication to anyone outside your business to ensure it does not contain any confusing jargon or acronyms.

- Ensure everyone working with you understands the current jargon and acronyms you use internally.

CHAPTER 10

DEAL WITH WHAT'S REAL

About 30 years ago when I was working at the National Australia Bank, it was about 11pm and I was coming up to the end of my shift. I was running some routine systems check when I inadvertently typed in the wrong command and started to shut down the bank's entire point of sale and ATM system. Everything went into slow motion and my heart started skipping beats.

I knew I only had minutes before the call centre was inundated with calls from angry customers who could not withdraw any money. I also knew the other computer operators would start to get red alert messages on the screens they were monitoring.

I took a few moments to stop swearing, start sweating and then do something about it. I immediately called the manager of the call centre and said, 'I've stuffed up and have brought the system down. You are about to get inundated with calls, but it should be back up in about 15 minutes'.

I then ran to my manager Rohan's office, yelling (while running) to my colleagues that I had mistakenly brought down the system across the country. I straightaway told my manager, 'I have made a big mistake'. And then I explained what I had done. I told him I had alerted the call centre and everyone who would be affected by my big stuff-up.

The system was restored and Rohan surprisingly seemed calm. In fact, he came over and thanked me for taking full accountability, responsibility and for acting fast.

It's important to note that I had a great working relationship with Rohan, so I didn't have any hesitation in telling him what had happened. He was an authentic leader who had created a culture of accountability, as opposed to one of blame and shame.

The point is that stuff-ups happen. They're part of what makes us real. They are also learning opportunities.

When you are prepared to take full responsibility and accountability quickly when mistakes happen, people tend to respond better. Authentic leadership is having the courage and confidence to accept the mistake with a genuine apology.

How we respond and deal with the stuff-ups is what counts in today's world.

Real-world problems

Miranda Kovacic is Domain Lead of Employee Experience at ANZ. She shared with me a mistake someone in her team made by sending out an email to 11 800 ANZ employees advising that they would be stopping the system that backed up emails. This created a lot of concern and calls, emails and texts soon came flooding in to Miranda.

Miranda knew she had to do something, and felt like she had three options. She could ignore the email, but she knew that was not great leadership; she could recall the email, which would not be a great message; or she could send a follow-up email. With the help of her communications advisor she sent the following email:

Recently we sent you an email about revoking your Personal Storage Tables. It was, and let's be honest here, a bit off the mark. As people have noted, it is with some irony that the update came from the Employee Experience domain.

I'm writing to you — and everyone we sent that email to — because my team and I recognise that that kind of email isn't especially helpful.

We'd like you to know we're working to include Human-Centered Design thinking into all our work…including opportunities to review existing processes.

And we're aiming for greater simplicity; our communications will be targeted, clear, timely…and ultimately more helpful.

In the interest of being fair to the team that sent the email, I'd like to mention that their efforts were well-intended. And they're certainly not the first team to have prematurely hit send on such an email.

Please ignore the original message; we're not revoking your access at this time. And know we're learning and improving day by day.

Miranda

Miranda sent that email at 3:22 pm, and four minutes later she had a response from Shayne Elliott, Chief Executive Officer of ANZ:

Wow — thank you Miranda and team — what a GREAT attitude to embrace feedback and make a commitment to improve.

I applaud your action and message.

Thanks!

Shayne

Miranda told me that her very first reaction was, 'WOW, how did he respond so quickly?' Her second reaction was that she felt really happy that he had taken the time to respond personally and positively.

Miranda told me she wanted the email to convey the cultural change underway at ANZ. To this day, she does not know which of her team sent the original email—because to her it didn't matter. What was important to her was 'how we responded'.

When you work in a culture where mistakes result in negative consequences, people will be very reluctant to admit mistakes. They will either try to hide what has happened or create excuses—rather than own up to them quickly and then try to fix them.

> *I can't emphasise enough the importance that the CEO or leader plays in creating a culture where dealing with what's real—mistake or otherwise—is encouraged and rewarded.*

Dealing with excuses

Remember the 2017 video of a man being forcibly removed from a United Airlines plane after the flight had been overbooked? David Dao, a 69-year-old doctor from Kentucky, was a passenger aboard that plane when United Airlines asked for volunteers to give up their seats. The airline said it needed the seats to accommodate extra crew members. Two passengers gave up their seats, but when Dao was asked, he declined.

So airline police physically dragged Dao out of his seat and down the aisle. Videos were taken by other passengers and the footage went viral on social media. Dao sustained concussion during the incident and was left with a broken nose and two lost teeth.

The company's first public statement included the line, 'We apologize for the overbook situation,' but they made no reference to Dr Dao or the video.

Later the same day, Chief Executive Officer Oscar Munoz released a statement calling the situation 'an upsetting event'. He apologised to the other passengers on the plane, but did not speak about Dao being forcibly removed. Munoz said:

> This is an upsetting event to all of us here at United. I apologize for having to re-accommodate these customers. Our team is moving with a sense of urgency to work with the authorities and conduct our own detailed review of what happened. We are also reaching out to this passenger to talk directly to him and further address and resolve this situation.

Later that evening a letter from Munoz was sent to United employees and it was later leaked and made public. In the letter, he told employees he stood by them and included a summary of the flight in which he described how staff first sought volunteers to give up their seats and then moved on to following their 'involuntary denial of boarding process', where staff pick who needs to leave the plane, along with in this case offering $1000 in compensation. According to Munoz, when Dao was approached, he refused to comply with instructions and vacate his seat. Munoz described that they were then forced to call in Chicago Aviation security officers to physically remove Dao—as he 'continued to resist' and act 'in defiance' of both airline crew and security staff. Munoz's description of Dao and of the event, seemed to contradict passenger descriptions of the incident, as well as the actual video footage.

The company's refusal to accept responsibility and offer a real apology to the victim resulted in a public relations nightmare.

Potential customers threatened to boycott the airline and an investigation was called for. Overnight, United Airlines stock plummeted by approximately 1 billion dollars in market value.

It was not until the following day that the company changed direction and, in a statement, Munoz took full responsibility.

> The truly horrific event that occurred on this flight has elicited many responses from all of us: outrage, anger, disappointment. I share all of those sentiments, and one above all: my deepest apologies for what happened. Like you, I continue to be disturbed by what happened on this flight and I deeply apologize to the customer forcibly removed and to all the customers aboard.
>
> No one should ever be mistreated this way.
>
> I want you to know that we take full responsibility and we will work to make it right.
>
> It's never too late to do the right thing. I have committed to our customers and our employees that we are going to fix what's broken so this never happens again. This will include a thorough review of crew movement, our policies for incentivizing volunteers in these situations, how we handle oversold situations and an examination of how we partner with airport authorities and local law enforcement. We'll communicate the results of our review by April 30th.
>
> I promise you we will do better.
>
> CEO Oscar Munoz

While offering excuses rather than apologies is often hugely tempting, blaming the victim in your excuses rarely ends well. In this case, the damage to brand, both personally to Munoz and to the company, would have been lessened if the last statement was the company's first.

Authentic leadership and dealing with what's real is not about plastic apologies—you know, the kinds of apologies that normally start with something like, 'If anyone was offended by my comments then I apologise'. Dealing with mistakes authentically is all about genuine apologies and communicating very clearly what action will be taken to fix the problem. Some people will feel so wronged and outraged that no amount of apologising will suffice. But the vast majority of people will respond positively to a genuine, heartfelt apology, especially when it is followed by a clear path of action.

Playing the blame game does more harm than good.

It's just not cricket

In March 2018, the Australian men's cricket team was touring South Africa on a test series. During the third test match, Cameron Bancroft, a relatively new member to the Australian team, was caught on camera rubbing the cricket ball with a small yellow object he had pulled out of his pocket. When Bancroft realised he had been seen, he hid the object down the front of his trousers.

When the umpires approached Bancroft and asked to see what was in his pocket, he responded by showing them the cloth used to clean his sunglasses, not the foreign object he had just placed down the front of his trousers.

At the press conference at the end of the day's play, Bancroft was accompanied by Australia's captain, Steve Smith. Both players acknowledged they had broken the rules by trying to alter the condition of the ball, but claimed they had used nothing more than adhesive tape with dirt stuck on it.

Both Smith and Bancroft seemed to underestimate the growing public reaction to what they had done. Bancroft was charged by the referee with a Level 2 offence, which included three demerit points and a fine of 75 per cent of his match payments. Smith was charged by the International Cricket Council with 'conduct of a serious nature that is contrary to the spirit of the game' and was banned for the next test match and forfeited

100 per cent of his match fee. Many fans in Australia—outraged by what they saw as straight-out cheating—thought more was needed.

It was not until five days later, after an investigation by Cricket Australia, that Bancroft admitted the foreign object was not just some adhesive tape, but actually sandpaper. As captain of the team, Smith admitted that he knew about the plan, which was hatched up during lunch by the 'leadership group'. Smith refused to name who was involved in this group.

Still seeming not to have grasped the seriousness of the event, Smith admitted it was a mistake, but said he had no plans to stand down as captain. Resentment and anger among the cricketing community then grew even further.

Cricket Australia launched a preliminary investigation, which resulted in an announcement that Smith, David Warner (the other player involved and vice-captain of the team) and Bancroft had been charged with bringing the game into disrepute and would be suspended from playing the final test match of the series and sent home.

The result of the full investigation? David Warner was found to be the plan's main instigator, instructing Bancroft on how to tamper with the ball. While on the field, Smith was found to have told Bancroft to hide the sandpaper in his trousers.

Warner was also found to have failed to prevent the plan being implemented, and to have misled match officials by concealing his knowledge of the plan and not voluntarily reporting his involvement. He received a 12-month suspension from all international and domestic cricket, with no consideration for team leadership positions in the future.

Smith was also found guilty of knowing about the plan and failing to take any action to prevent it. He misled match officials and made misleading public comments regarding the nature of the plan and who was involved. He received a 12-month suspension from all international and domestic cricket, with no consideration for team leadership positions until a minimum of 12 months after his suspension.

Bancroft also received a 9-month suspension from all international and domestic cricket, with no consideration for team leadership positions until a minimum of 12 months after the conclusion of his suspension.

The same day, the Board of Control for Cricket in India announced that neither Smith nor Warner would be able to play in the 2018 International Premier League. While in England, Somerset, where Bancroft had been recruited to play in the County Championship season, announced that he would no longer be playing for them.

Upon their return home to Australia, all three players held emotional press conferences, breaking down and apologising unashamedly for their actions. The seriousness of what they had done seemed to have finally sunk in.

As captain of the Australian cricket team, Smith took full responsibility, and said he had made a serious error in judgement, adding, 'It was a failure of leadership, my leadership'. As well as apologising to his 'teammates, to fans of cricket all over the world and to all Australians who are disappointed and angry,' he specifically referred to the effect the incident had had on his parents. He added, 'I know I will regret this for the rest of my life. I'm absolutely gutted. I hope in time I can earn back respect and forgiveness'.

Australia's coach Darren Lehmann was cleared by the investigation of playing any part in the scandal. He said he was embarrassed and disappointed, but he would not resign. However, after viewing the press conference of the players, he announced that he would step down from his role as coach.

The commercial fallout of the ball-tampering scandal was unprecedented—for both Cricket Australia and the individual players concerned. One of Cricket Australia's major sponsors, the Magellan Financial Group, terminated its three-year sponsorship agreement in response. The contract had two more seasons to run, and was estimated to be worth approximately AU$20 million.

On an individual sponsorship level for the players in question, LG announced that they would not renew their personal sponsorship of Warner. The sporting apparel company ASICS terminated their commercial arrangements with Warner and Bancroft. The Commonwealth Bank and Sanitarium both terminated their sponsorship of Smith.

While the three players involved will most likely play cricket for Australia again, it is hard to see their reputation ever fully recovering from this incident.

Some would argue that the reactions and fines did not match the crime. I would suggest that the public's and Cricket Australia's reactions were so severe because the players had betrayed the trust of the Australian public.

There is an important lesson here for us all.

As leaders, we will always be judged on our actions and decisions—and that comes with a cost.

This cost might be a literal, immediate financial cost, but you've also got to consider the overall damage to your brand. This kind of intangible cost is very hard to win back.

A fucking monumental stuff-up

I introduced Kate Hughes in the previous chapter. Before taking on her current role at RMIT, she was Chief Risk Officer at one of Australia's largest telephone and mobile network providers. One night, during the nightly news, Kate was on live TV being interviewed about a major security breach that had taken place several times over the previous few months.

The company she worked for had inadvertently listed the private numbers of some of their customers. These were people who, in some cases, had fled from domestic violence situations and were in hiding from their abusive partners.

Several aspects struck me about Kate's responses to the interviewer's questions. The very first question they asked was, 'What happened?'

Kate responded with, 'We stuffed up. And we didn't stuff up once, we stuffed up several times'.

She then went on to talk about how unacceptable the breach was. How she had spoken to the customers affected and how they were changing systems and processes to ensure it would not happen again.

I called Kate the next day to commend her on her real responses, especially the 'stuff-up' comment. It turned out her CEO was out of the country and the company's head of media thought Kate would be the best person to face the press.

Kate told me she'd said she would agree to do the interview on one condition: she was not going to make excuses for what had happened because 'it was a fucking monumental stuff-up'. The head of media had looked at her and said, 'Okay, but can you not say "fucking" and can you not say "monumental"?'

Dealing with what's real is not about demolishing all boundaries but about making smart and conscious choices.

Kate demonstrated courage through being prepared to deal with what was real and admit the stuff-up. She had congruence with her own personal values. She told me that she had a pact with her husband (also a chief risk officer) to always speak the truth.

Your feet need to follow your mouth

Dealing with a scandal often needs to start with an immediate and heartfelt apology. Depending on the level of the scandal or the number of misdeeds, dealing with that reality can be a long-term process. SNC-Lavalin, the largest engineering firm in Canada, experienced this a few years ago.

Founded in 1911, SNC-Lavalin has offices in over 50 countries and operations in over 160. From 2011 to 2013, the company experienced a series of corruption allegations, including:

- *2011:* One of the vice presidents was investigated on a range of corruption and financial fraud charges (he eventually pleaded guilty).

- *2012:* Then CEO Pierre Duhaime resigned and was arrested 9 months later by the Quebec authorities on charges of fraud, conspiracy to commit fraud and the use of false documents. (At the time of writing, his case is still before the courts.)

- *2013:* Former executives were accused of providing an improper $22 million payment to the CEO of the McGill University Health Centre, connected to the bidding process for construction of their new hospital. The CEO died before he could stand trial, but his wife pleaded guilty to money laundering.

Some of SNC-Lavalin's executives had also formed close relationships with Muammar Gaddafi's regime in Libya and, when the regime fell, they left a reported $23 million dollars behind in Libyan banks as well as evidence of corrupt dealings with the Gaddafi family itself.

This sounds bad, and it is, but it got worse. In 2013, the World Bank blacklisted 250 companies from bidding on their global projects due to an investigation relating to the Padma Bridge project in Bangladesh. Of the 250 blacklisted companies, 117 were Canadian, with SNC-Lavalin and its affiliate partners comprising115 of the 117.

Not surprisingly, the company's stock price hit a low of $37 in January 2016, down from a high of $61 in early 2011.

In an interview with Patricia Alleyn, SNC-Lavalin's Head of Integrity Program, she described the events during those two years as a 'tornado of scandals'. In the end, all of SNC-Lavalin's employees felt they were being tarnished by the actions of a few previous senior executives. They experienced scrutiny and criticism not only from the press and on social media, but also from their friends and family — at backyard barbeques, and their children's soccer games for example.

Patricia explained they 'lost a lot of good people'. Special communication channels were set up to keep employees informed of what was happening and what was going to happen. Despite these efforts, she explained that due to the legal circumstances, communications couldn't be as expansive or detailed as one wanted. However, after a period of time, and based on employee and public reaction to this approach, it became clear that communications to employees and external stakeholders had to be completely transparent if SNC-Lavalin was going to move on from these scandals.

Under the leadership of the newly created role of Chief Compliance Officer, the company turned to International regulations to develop and implement a comprehensive Ethics & Compliance program. Rolled out across the company and including a revised code of conduct, training, a hotline and other measures, this program reached every employee and focused on transparency and doing the right thing. The high standard to which SNC-Lavalin's program is held is evidenced by an assessment done last summer by Transparency International. Transparency International (UK) is a global organisation that works with governments and businesses to help fight corruption, and following their assessment, they noted that SNC-Lavalin had taken actions to become even more transparent than many of their peers, such as developing an annual report on lobbying and political activities which is shared on their website.

As Patricia explained to me, authentic communication and leadership is not shown in one single action; it needs to be continuous and evolving.

Apologising and taking accountability needs to happen quickly, but that on its own is not enough—you need to show you are taking action to ensure it doesn't happen again.

As Head of the Integrity Program Office, Patricia continues to refine the program by implementing company-wide initiatives such as the Code of Conduct training, wherein employees are taken through a variety of real-life examples from within their company and the industry to help guide them in their future behaviours and choices.

While this training occurs across the company, other mandatory training is focused on middle management and business development because this is where the pressure to deliver results can be higher and also where inappropriate activities can most readily occur. These targeted trainings raise awareness that, as individuals, these people are responsible for making ethical choices and are ultimately accountable for them. They are reminded that it is not only the company's reputation at risk but also their own.

The company culture supports employees in reporting any instances in which they think the Code of Conduct was not followed. To be true to its promise of transparent communication, SNC-Lavalin updates their trainings regularly to include internal examples based on these instances so that the trainings are relevant to the state of the business and also to shape behaviours in potentially problematic areas.

Employees, including senior executives, are also being assessed on their compliance to the Code of Conduct and, in some cases, have been terminated for not living up to the standards. The company also requires business partners to follow the Code of Conduct and has ceased dealing with certain organisations whose behaviour did not adhere to the Code of Conduct.

Patricia explained that these actions were critical to ensure the scandals did not happen again. She explained the French saying 'vos pieds doivent suivre votre parole', which basically translates to 'your feet need to follow your mouth'. Others would say 'actions speak louder than words' or 'walk the talk, not just talk the talk'. Either way you look at it, dealing with the reality of scandal is all about taking accountability followed by action and communicating that in a transparent and authentic way. The impact of this approach was that following a 2017 exercise with employees to determine the company's values, Integrity was chosen to be one of the four core values.

When looking for advice on telling the truth or not, we can always look to the wisdom of Mark Twain, who wrote, 'When in doubt tell the truth'. Although not in the original text, many sources add, 'It will confound your enemies and astound your friends'.

Get REAL now

- Ditch the plastic apologies when a mistake has been made and make a quick and genuine apology instead.

- Follow any apology with genuine action.

- Create a culture where mistakes are seen as learning opportunities so your team feels safe to admit mistakes.

- Understand how hard it can be to rebuild trust once it is lost.

CHAPTER 11

SHOW WHAT'S REAL TO YOU

In a 2018 *Harvard Business Review* article 'The New CEO Activists', authors Aaron Chatterji and Michael Toffel reported that more CEOs are breaking from tradition and taking a stand on divisive social issues.

The report only focused on the United States, but some examples highlighted include:

- Dan Schulman of PayPal taking a stand against a North Carolina law firm that required people to use the bathrooms that corresponded with the gender on their birth certificate.

- Goldman Sachs CEO, Lloyd Blankfein, speaking out publicly about LGBTQ rights.

- Bill Oesterle, former CEO of Angie's List, cancelling a planned expansion into Indianapolis in response to Indiana's Religious Freedom Restoration Act (which many viewed as anti-LGBTQ rights).

- Salesforce CEO Marc Benioff threatening to stop all employees travelling to Indiana in reaction to the same bill.

- The CEOs of 14 major food companies—including Mars, Coco-Cola, Unilever and PepsiCo—all co-signing an open letter for government leaders to 'meaningfully address the reality of climate change' days before the United Nations climate change agreement in Paris in late 2015.

- Over 100 CEOs co-signing an amicus brief to have President Trump's 2017 executive order to ban citizens from seven Muslims countries entering the United States overturned.

While traditionally CEOs and other business leaders may have done nothing or adopted non-confrontational tactics, such as lobbying behind the scenes or contributing to campaigns, more and more are taking more active roles. This includes raising awareness via social media statements or writing opinion pieces, as well as exerting economic influence by relocating business activities or funding political and activist groups.

Chatterji and Toffel concluded this has occurred due to frustration with the growing political turmoil and paralysis in government. And because CEOs are realising that the more they speak up on social issues, the more they will be expected to in the future.

Even stakeholders are starting to expect corporate leaders to take a stand and speak out.

In January 2019, mining companies Rio Tinto and BHP released a joint statement calling for an Indigenous voice in the Australian Federal Parliament to act as an advisory board and commission to oversee treaty-making and truth-telling. With BHP CEO, Andrew Mackenzie stating 'we cannot stand on the sidelines'.

As Salesforce CEO Marc Benioff told *Time*, 'Todays CEOs need to stand up not just for their shareholders, but their employees, their customers, their partners, the community, the environment. Schools, everybody'.

Australia takes to the skies

In 2017, legalising same-sex marriage was a hot political topic in Australia. A plebiscite was conducted via a non-compulsory postal vote to see what the Australian public wanted. People were asked to vote yes if they wanted same-sex marriage to be legalised, or no if they disagreed.

People took to the skies, paying for planes to write YES or NO in the air, while others turned to media campaigns, talkback radio shows and TV to voice their opinion. It was a highly emotional time!

Alan Joyce, Chief Executive of Qantas, Australia's biggest airline, made a public stand on the issue. Joyce was so vocal towards the yes vote that it even led to a disgruntled man smashing a meringue pie into Joyce's face during a public speech. Joyce (who is an openly gay man) was also criticised by members of parliament, who said he should not use his company's brand to campaign on the issue.

Joyce was undeterred and continued to campaign for yes, even donating $1 million of his own money to the campaign. He was joined by over 20 high-profile chief executives of some of Australia's largest companies, all offering their support for same-sex marriage.

Joyce echoed the sentiments of Salesforce's Benioff when he said, 'I think it is very important for our employees, customers and our shareholders, and that is why Qantas is a supporter of marriage equality and a supporter of gender equality and a supporter of Indigenous rights'.

Ironically, the Deputy Prime Minister at the time, Barnaby Joyce (no relation to Alan), who opposed gay marriage and argued it was against traditional family values, was later revealed to have been conducting an extramarital affair. He later left his wife of 24 years and four daughters. He was slammed in the media, and by the general public and yes voters for being a hypocrite.

To be an authentic leader, your actions must match your words.

Fighting for 'traditional family values' at the same time as having an affair is, not surprisingly, going to go down like a lead balloon. Three months after the deciding vote, same-sex marriage became legal in all Australian states and territories. Just weeks later, Barnaby Joyce resigned from his ministerial and leadership roles after he admitted the woman he was having an affair with was an ex-staffer and they were expecting a baby.

Authentic leaders are congruent in what they personally believe in their private life and how they lead in their professional life and in the public arena.

A new zeal

Showing what is real to you relates not only to the words you use but also to your actions and decisions. Authentic leaders show congruence in what they say and what they do. Take Jacinda Ardern, for example, who became New Zealand's 40th Prime Minister in 2017.

Becoming prime minister at the age of 37 made her the world's youngest female head of government. When she gave birth to her first child in June 2018, she became the world's second elected head of government to have a baby while in office. (The only other world leader to give birth while in office was former Pakistani Prime Minister Benzir Bhutto, in 1990.)

Ardern has also been a strong supporter of parental leave and working mothers. A few months after giving birth, she appeared on a global stage with her young daughter at the United Nations General Assembly in New York.

This received global media attention, but in a CNN interview at the time Ardern said, 'I want to normalise it,' going on to say, 'If we want to make workplaces more open, we need to acknowledge logistical challenges... By being more open it might create a path for other women'.

Ardern has also shown congruence in other issues she supports. She has a reputation of being a frugal leader and not wasting taxpayers' money. While in New York, her partner also travelled to the UN General Assembly to take care of their daughter, Neve. Because no spousal program was available to cover the costs of her partner's travel, Ardern said they made a judgement call to pay for these out of their own personal funds.

In 2018 she also froze MPs salaries for a year, and insists her ministers carpool to events whenever possible.

Ardern has shown congruence in what she says and what she does. Compare this to Barnaby Joyce taking a stand on 'traditional marriage values' while having an affair—creating a total incongruence between his words and actions.

Your 'version 2.0'

In 2012, ex-Australian rules footballer Nathan Buckley took over as senior coach of Collingwood as part of their succession planning. At the time, the club had no problems, having finished top of the ladder the previous two years and winning the Grand Final in 2010.

Yet by 2017, after five years of the club finishing below expectations, people were suggesting Buckley should be sacked as coach. Under growing pressure, the club announced a review of all personnel.

Buckley made it through the review and maintained his role as senior coach. In 2018 Collingwood finished third on the ladder and made it through to the Grand Final, which they ended up losing by five points. However, much of the commentary was focused on Buckley's transformation as a leader. Many called it 'Buckley version 2.0'.

In an interview the week before the 2018 Grand Final, Buckley revealed he'd realised he needed to be a more authentic leader. He said, 'Becoming more authentic and becoming more real was an important part, even internally, of me enjoying myself more'.

He also discussed the importance of speaking about what was important to him, believing that being 'a bit more expressive is more real'. And he suggested that we should 'just say what's on your mind. Speak from the heart and see where it goes'.

Buckley outlined he had been living his life how others expected him to live it—as the tough, unrelenting coach. When he realised he needed to live life how he wanted and not how others expected him to act, it was 'liberating'. Stating that, 'when you give yourself a licence to be more of yourself, you actually find out a little bit more about what makes you tick. About what you love and what you hate. It allows you to actually feel real'.

Buckley talked about how he no longer fixated on the little things that went wrong but instead focused on the 95 per cent that went right. And at the Grand Final in 2018, the biggest day of his coaching career, he showed this new leadership style at two significant moments.

The first was the Collingwood banner being torn to shreds by wind just moments before the team took to the ground. Buckley could see members of the Collingwood cheer squad (responsible for the banner) becoming distraught, with one woman in tears. Even though he was about to coach the most important game of his career, which had now been marred by a 'bad omen', Buckley went over to the woman and hugged her.

During the game, Collingwood runner Alex Woodward inadvertently got in the way of a Collingwood player, preventing him from marking the ball. This resulted in an opposition player taking the mark and kicking a goal (significant considering the game was decided by less than a goal).

A visibly distraught Woodward was in tears in the dressing room after the game when again Buckley hugged him and consoled him with words of encouragement.

His actions backed his words — by not focusing on what went wrong.

Yet taking a stand and showing what is real for you is not just the domain of CEOs, political leaders or senior coaches.

You don't need a leadership title (or an acronym after your name) to take a stance and show up as real.

Who is in your corner of the court?

Rachana Bhide is a business psychologist with 19 years' experience as a consulting and talent leader. At the time of writing, she is the Global Talent leader for 5000-plus software and infrastructure engineers in New York City, working for one of the US's leading financial companies.

Rachana also has a side passion. She is obsessed about gender equality, but believes that for too long men have not been included in these conversations. Instead of shaming men, her belief is that they need to know they are part of the solution.

In 2015, while undertaking a master's in organisational psychology at Columbia University, she completed her thesis—titled 'Engaging Men in Diversity Initiatives'. Her research showed three key findings:

1. Men who reflected on their own life experiences were stronger and more authentic allies for diversity.

2. Storytelling was a compelling and proven method for helping men articulate their commitment.

3. Positive psychology helped build self-confidence of men to be better allies, thus influencing behaviour change.

A few months later Rachana was asked to give a presentation on her research at a gala held by Women in Sports and Events — The Women of Inspiration Awards in Los Angeles. She wanted to start her presentation with her own personal story of a male ally. This is the story she told:

    It was an extremely hot August afternoon in Virginia. I had spent the summer on the tennis court, training for our hometown tennis team. My older brother Jeet, a state champion tennis player, had spent the summer as my coach. It was time for my next match of the tournament, which would be an easy match except for one thing: I was 12 years old and had a huge crush on the boy, Evan, who I was set to play against.

    I looked across the net before the match started. Evan smiled at me. I knew Evan liked me back...but I also knew I could beat him. As I stood at the baseline before making my first serve, I seriously asked myself:

    'Do I let him win?'

    It was the first time in my life that I became aware of gender and the potential roles you need to play. I can recall thinking that if I like this boy, which I did and I wanted him to like me, then perhaps I should let him win.

    I looked to the corner of the court and saw Jeet, my tennis coach and champion, who had always encouraged me to play my best and play to win. I decided I would not let him down, and I beat Evan...easily, in straight sets.

    I walked off the court. And Evan never spoke to me again, let alone smiled at me.

At that critical moment, at 12 years old, I had been faced with a choice I'd encounter time and again...But I knew I'd made the right decision. I had played my hardest, rather than holding back.

And more so, I knew that Jeet was and would always be my biggest champion, on and off the court. He was my first male ally and he was in my corner.

Rachana's story of her brother is a powerful one, but it is what happened next that convinced her to speak out more about her passion.

Before presenting in Los Angeles, she thought she would let Jeet know that she was sharing a story about him. When she told him the story he was genuinely shocked. He'd had no idea that his actions and his words of encouragement on the tennis court that day had such an impact on her life (and he certainly had no idea that his little 12-year-old sister had a crush on that boy).

Rachana realised that it had taken her 25 years to tell her own brother the importance and long-lasting impact his support had provided her. She saw that sharing her story about her brother would not only encourage him to proactively seek out opportunities to support other women in his life (personally and professionally), but also, and more importantly, encourage other men to realise that they can make a difference.

Rachana had discovered in her research that a lot of men who were not in a position of authority disconnected from the gender equality conversation because they thought they were not able to make a difference. So she created a website called 'The Corner of the Court Project', a reference and tribute to her brother Jeet, where women are encouraged to share their personal stories of male allies.

Rachana didn't receive any push back or resistance about the project—until 18 months after the launch of the website when the #METOO movement hit. She was conscious of not wanting to dilute the significance and integrity of the #METOO message. She also thought that people at this point in time may not want to hear the positive stories of men supporting women. It was only after a few months of deliberation, and with encouragement from her colleagues and friends, that she realised these positive stories were exactly what needed to be added to the movement.[1]

---

[1] If you want to submit a story about how a male ally has supported you, go to cornerofthecourt.com/.

Of course, you don't need to make your own website to speak up about what is real for you. Anyone can exercise leadership, and you don't need a title or platform.

For example, my 15-year-old daughter, Jess, wanted to raise awareness at her school about the impact plastic straws were having on the environment. She moulded a turtle from clay, painted it and stuck a straw down its nostril to highlight that this is sometimes where straws end up. She then asked permission to place it in her school canteen.

You can display leadership in any cause that's important to you. If you think you can make a difference, speak up and show what's real for you.

The consequences of speaking up

Taking a stand always includes the risk of consequences. Sometimes you may be aware of potential consequences and be prepared to take the risk; other times the consequences can be a complete surprise.

Early in 2018, Tasmania's last abortion provider closed down, which meant that while abortion was legal in Tasmania, women had no access to the providers to undertake the procedure. This resulted in Tasmanian women having no other choice but to travel interstate to have a surgical abortion.

At the time, Angela Williamson, one of the first women in Tasmania forced to fly to Melbourne for an abortion, was working as a manager of public policy and government relations for Tasmania at Cricket Australia. Having worked in politics previously, however, she used her media contacts to speak up for Tasmanian women. She also took to social media, tweeting about women's rights to safe and accessible abortion procedures.

During the state election campaign, the Labor opposition, led by Rebecca White, announced their policy that the abortion procedure be performed in the Tasmanian public hospital system. At a Liberal election announcement, the policy was not backed by the government. Williamson took to Twitter again, directing one particular tweet to the premier:

> Did he forget his words and actions have an impact? Did he forget that patients of this service are f*****g vulnerable. That his words can harm. Most irresponsible, gutless and reckless delivery in party ever.

She was subsequently sacked by her employer at the time, Cricket Australia. A statement put out by the company said, 'Cricket Australia respects an individual's right to their opinion. However, it expects that employees will refrain from making offensive comments that contravene the organisation's policies'.

Williamson is now suing Cricket Australia for unfair dismissal. A statement put out by her lawyer argues,

> The Fair Work Act says you can't be sacked for your political opinion. That's what Angela did, she expressed her political opinion in her tweet, and then she subsequently found herself being sacked from her job at Cricket Australia. It seems extraordinary that someone would be sacked from their job in those circumstances. Her job at Cricket Australia had nothing to do with the public debate around access to reproductive health services in Tasmania.

At the time of writing, Williamson is maintaining her campaign to ensure all women in Australia have access to safe and affordable contraception and pregnancy terminations.

Regardless of whether or not you agree with Williamson or the way she went about expressing her opinion, there were certainly consequences for her taking a stand and speaking up. Only she can determine if the consequences were worth it.

In a TV interview a few months later, Williamson said she should not have sworn in the tweet, but she does not regret the intent of the tweet. In September 2018 Williamson reached a confidential out-of-court settlement with Cricket Australia.

The spice of life

Tracey Spicer was a TV newsreader throughout the 1990s and 2000s for Australia's Network Ten, and was later an international anchor for Sky News. She is now a highly sought-after keynote speaker and media commentator.

In 2017 she published *The Good Girl Stripped Bare* after her highly successful TEDx Talk 'The Lady Stripped Bare' in 2014. On Australia Day in 2018 she was appointed as a Member of the Order of Australia for 'significant service to the broadcast media as a journalist and television presenter, and as an ambassador for social welfare and charitable groups'. Later that same year Spicer was named winner in the social enterprise and not-for-profit category of *The Australian Financial Review* 100 Women of Influence awards.

Spicer's most public speak out moment came in 2017 after the #METOO movement rocked the American film and TV industry. Spicer waited for similar revelations to come from Australia. Having worked in this industry all her career, she knew it was rife with similar stories of sexual harassment and assault. So she waited for someone to break the ice in Australia and take the lead... and waited.

She then realised that the person to break the ice needed to be her. Spicer felt she had 'no choice' about taking action for several reasons.

Firstly, she felt guilty that she knew of this sexual harassment in her own industry but had never really done anything about it, except fight her own battles. She also knew that due to her experience and skills she was well placed to take the lead on this. And she felt it was a once in a lifetime opportunity to make a difference on the back of the momentum of the #METOO movement.

Her taking a stand started with her tweet at 8:34 am on 18 October, 2017: 'Currently, I am investigating two long-term offenders in our media industry. Please, contact me privately to tell your stories'.

Hundreds of women contacted Spicer, sharing their experiences of injustice. Spicer asked if they wanted counselling, legal or police support, before requesting they speak off the record or on camera.

Spicer's initial tweet and a subsequent investigation, in collaboration with Fairfax Media and the ABC, resulted in some high-profile cases of men in the Australian media industry being accused of systemic sexual harassment. The investigation has since won two Walkley Awards. (These awards celebrate excellence in journalism.)

Since Spicer's initial tweet, over 2200 people have come forward to share their stories of harassment and abuse.

When speaking with these victims, Spicer saw a common theme on why so many did not initially speak up. Many said they knew they would not be believed or feared being sacked. Some even did not speak up because they felt sorry for the perpetrators.

As a result of her investigations, Spicer received death and rape threats, and threats directed towards her and her family.

As shocking as these threats are, Spicer shared with me that the backlash is exactly what she expected. She knew from her personal experience that 'when you speak on issues that affect the gender power balance there will always be consequences and backlash'. Yet she was willing to take the risk.

To stand or not to stand?

With potential consequences like those discussed in the previous sections, you may think saying nothing and staying in neutral territory is the best option for everyone. Yet Professor Aaron Chatterji of Duke University's Fuqua School of Business disagrees.

In his studies of CEO activism, he has found that 'being in the neutral middle, where most companies used to be a generation ago, is no longer tenable' adding that 'it is seen as lacking authenticity'.

Another study—'CEO Activism in 2017: High Noon in the C-Suite', conducted in 2017 by Weber Shandwick and KRC Research—revealed that almost half (47 per cent) of millennials surveyed believe that CEOs should take a public stand on social issues. This percentage dropped to 28 per cent for those in generation X and baby boomers.

The report also found that over half (51 per cent) of millennials are more likely to buy from companies if their CEO speaks out on issues. This is an 11 per cent increase on the previous year's data. The figure again drops for those in generation X to 33 per cent and for baby boomers to 30 per cent.

Finally, the research showed that 47 per cent of people surveyed say CEOs who do not speak out risk criticism, whether from the media, customers, employees or the government, and 21 per cent say silent CEOs risk declining sales.

Other CEOs I know have actively made a choice not to take a stand on social issues. While they support particular causes personally, they feel like taking a stand in their official role as CEO is unfair to the employees who work for them who do not support the cause or, in fact, have opposing views.

This argument is valid.

Chris Freund, who I introduced in chapter 9, is one such CEO. Chris has strong personal values on some controversial social issues. For example, he believes that drug use should be decriminalised around the world. As head of Mekong Capital, he has made a decision not to connect his personal views with the company.

He knows that not all employees and other stakeholders would agree and does not want to force his views onto them. He feels doing so would be unfair and, therefore, finds ways to contribute to his causes in other more personal ways.

Showing what is real to you doesn't have to involve a public stand. Consequences always come from that, so only you can decide on what action you take. Authentic leadership does, however, require congruence between what you say and what you do, and between the values you adhere to in your personal life and in your professional life.

Remember, you don't need a leadership title to show leadership and what's real to you.

Get REAL now

- Be consistent with the way you act at home and at work.

- Ensure your words and actions are congruent.

- Take a public stand if that is important for you.

- Seek council to understand any potential consequences of your actions before you take them.

CHAPTER 12

KNOW WHAT'S REAL FOR OTHERS

'It's not you, it's me'... Have you ever said those words or had them said to you during a relationship break-up? When we say these words, we are in a place of self-preservation. We don't really want to tell the other person we have fallen out of love with them and so we avoid that difficult conversation and the potential backlash that might follow.

Our natural survival instinct is to keep ourselves from danger, and dealing with an upset and emotional person screaming, 'What do you mean you don't love me anymore?' is as big a threat as any.

These same survival instincts are present at work. Our desire to keep the peace is what holds us back from giving feedback to our peers and our team. When it comes to giving feedback to more senior people, the survival instinct is stronger than ever, even when we are asked for our feedback.

Every time we ask for feedback we are competing with the in-built human DNA of self-preservation.

Without real feedback, however, addressing issues, improving performance and generally making progress can be difficult.

Politeness prolongs progress

Mark LeBusque is a speaker, coach and author of *Being Human*, published in 2017. Mark believes that in order to make real progress, humans must be able to speak their truth without fear or favour.

Mark works with organisations around the world to do this by helping them embrace a more authentic way of working, and helping employees step into authentic leadership regardless of their authority.

I first met Mark in 2014 when we both attended an Adaptive Leadership Executive Education program at Harvard I instantly liked Mark for his transparency, ability to say it as it is and, at times, disruptive humour. It is no surprise that we bonded with each other instantly.

Mark strongly believes that politeness prolongs progress. He argues we have been practising the art of politeness and not speaking truth to power since we were children. We told our parents what they wanted to hear at home and we told our teachers what they wanted to hear at school.

When we enter the workforce, the practice of politeness is no different. The very hierarchical nature of organisations often means that, as 'subordinates', we assume a reduced level of power and tell leaders what they want to hear and not what they need to hear.

Mark's point is that 'the DNA that made us run away from sabre-toothed tigers[1] is the same DNA that makes us run away from difficult conversations'.

But even though we are competing against our DNA, we can mitigate this response. The following sections discuss some useful methods.

---

[1] Sabre-toothed tigers get a really bad rap in the retelling of history.

Power to the person

Research conducted in 2014 and led by Elizabeth Morrison (Professor of Management and Vice Dean of Faculty at New York University, Stern School of Business) looked into why employees choose to stay silent instead of reporting a problem, expressing a different opinion or offering a suggestion.

Morrison, along with her colleagues Kelly See of NYU Stern and Caitlin Pan of Singapore's SIM University, used a set of three studies to conduct the research. One was laboratory-based and two were survey-based.

Their theory was that silence is driven by a lower sense of personal power. According to this theory, a heightened sense of personal power results in the person being more confident, ruled by positive emotions, and behaving with fewer inhibitions. On the other hand, a person with a perceived lower sense of power has reduced confidence and optimism, is driven by anxiety and other negative emotions, is more aware of potential risks and threats, and is inhibited in social situations. In the workplace, the end result is employee silence.

The research supported this theory, showing that a key contributing factor to employees staying silent is their perception of having little power in relation to others at work. However, their research also found that this effect of feeling powerless is significantly reduced when the employee regards their leader as open to input.

Regardless of your seniority, you have probably experienced this situation firsthand. I know a lot of the people I speak to tell me they do not have a problem speaking up in front of their team or peers but struggle to do this in more senior forums. Their perception of less personal power results in them being silent or at least reluctant to voice a differing opinion or offer a suggestion. Self-preservation kicks in.

In times of change and uncertainty, and especially in times of restructures and job insecurities, this self-preservation kicks in quicker and with more people. Employees who would normally speak up are suddenly quiet.

I see and hear of this at some of the most senior levels in organisations. A client of mine, Anton, worked for a great CEO, whom Anton described as one of the most transparent leaders he had worked with. The CEO actively sought out feedback and took it on board.

However, during a recent time of significant change, Anton noticed that some members of the executive leadership team stopped voicing their differing opinions and concerns in front of the CEO but would do so when the CEO was not around. Anton could see that, in some cases, this was undermining (deliberately or not) other members of the team and the CEO himself. And it was not only Anton noticing this but also other leaders in the company.

At about this time, Anton was moved onto another project and the CEO asked him for feedback—specifically asking him to tell him what others perhaps would not be prepared to. So Anton did tell him what he had observed with the team. The CEO was genuinely shocked and dismayed that no-one had spoken to him directly. He was even more disappointed that so many people knew about these comments but none were prepared to tell him.

The reality is that, just like Anton, they were reluctant—even with a leader who had a great reputation of receiving feedback positively. If reluctance can occur in these positive conditions and at a very senior level, then it is almost a given that reluctance to speak the truth at lower levels down the organisation will be higher. And that this reluctance will be even higher in times of change and when the leader is not actively creating a culture of openness.

Leaders need to increase their openness, especially during times of change, so employees feel more power to provide feedback, voice differing opinions and offer suggestions.

Ask the question and hold the silence

When you ask for feedback or ask for others' opinions, be prepared to hold the (inevitable) silence. Too often leaders ask for questions and after a second of silence proclaim, 'Great! No questions, meeting over'. The reality is we all are not comfortable with silence so the moment the silence feels awkward we start talking.

Real open leaders hold this silence and are aware when everyone in the room is simply nodding away in agreement.

Mark LeBusque believes we need to move beyond empowering people to creating permission for them to speak out. He argues asking 'any questions?' is not granting permission; you need to go deeper than that. Try asking something like, 'What's going on in the room right now? I feel everyone is agreeing with me but I am concerned no differing opinions have been heard'.

One technique that I have seen work when asking the team for feedback is to allow everyone to speak before responding to feedback. Hold the silence until everyone in the team has contributed. This may even involve specifically asking some people for their feedback (perhaps from your junior introverted staff).

This can be a challenge because your natural tendency is likely to want to respond to every piece of feedback as it comes up, and in some instances defend it. The moment you become defensive with one piece of feedback, however, others will become reluctant to speak up.

During my training at Harvard undertaking the Adaptive Leadership program, I experienced firsthand how challenging not immediately responding to feedback can be. In a small group activity called the Leadership Challenge, we were asked to present a challenge we had to our group. We were allocated ten minutes to explain the challenge, and the group then had another ten minutes to ask clarifying questions about the challenge. Then you had to turn your back on your group while they spent 15 minutes talking about what they thought was really going on. You were not allowed to say anything during this time.

This was one of the most challenging leadership development activities I have ever done. The temptation to defend myself or correct them was excruciating. But my enforced silence meant that feedback and suggestions flowed from the rest of the group. And the process ended up providing me with some of the biggest insights into my leadership and behaviour I have ever received. I truly believe those insights would not have come if I had been able to speak during those 15 minutes.

If you really want to know what is real for your people, learn to hold the silence—however uncomfortable it feels.

Listen and learn

Michael Young, a senior leader at Cigna, one of America's largest health insurance services providers, is known as a great listener.

Michael believes that the only way you can really get to know what is going on with the people you lead is to spend time with them. He says, 'When you give people your most precious resource, time, they appreciate it. And when it is genuine and you are fully present, it builds trust and loyalty'. Michael makes a point of scheduling time in his diary to be out talking with his employees, especially when he travels to different site locations.

What he has learnt over his more than 30-year career is not only the importance of listening but also the power in the questions you ask. Like Mark, he referred to asking questions that provide genuine permission. He explains this further by saying that if you just ask people 'How are you?' or 'How's things?', 90 per cent of people will respond with a 'fine' or 'okay'. As the research mentioned earlier in this chapter has proven, the very nature of the pecking order in organisations creates a reluctance to speak the truth without permission.

The questions you ask need to provide permission. So instead of asking for general feedback, Michael says he will ask questions like, 'No matter how well you think we are doing, what is one thing you think we could do differently?'

Give people real permission to speak the truth.

Show you care

Michael also believes that you need to genuinely care for people for them to open up to you more readily.

For example, Michael once had a young graduate called Logan who was a good worker. One day Logan came to Michael advising him that he was leaving to go work for his parents in their family business. Michael could tell he was uneasy and, after some more questions, uncovered that Logan really didn't want to leave but was succumbing to family pressures. Michael also felt that the role Logan was going into didn't seem to match his interests, capabilities or potential.

Respecting Logan's wishes and his family's, Michael simply wrote his phone number and email address on a piece of paper and asked Logan to call if he ever needed to. He also suggested they meet up in a couple of months. He also advised Logan that if his new role did not work out, he could return to Cigna at any time.

A couple of months later, Logan did call Michael advising the role wasn't working out and his parents had agreed he should go back to the job he loved. Logan returned to Cigna and Michael advised that he works harder and has more loyalty than ever before.

Connect and contribute

Stephen Purcell also understands the importance of spending time with his employees to create a genuine connection. Stephen shared a story with me that occurred when he was Managing Partner of a firm that had 300 to 400 people. He was at a function with several other managing partners of firms of a similar size. Stephen shared with the group his practice of having a 30-minute meeting with every new employee who starts with his firm. He was shocked by the almost unison response of, 'Why would you bother doing that?'

Stephen's reaction was, 'Why would you *not* do this?' Stephen cannot think of a better use of his time as Managing Partner. And he is not doing it just to be a nice guy and provide a feel-good experience. He knows that when you build a genuine connection with people, they are more likely to approach you with feedback and suggestions. Stephen argues, 'Everyone wants to do their best at work and my job is to figure out how I can help them do that. If a stronger connection to me helps that, then I will do it'.

He believes that a leader creating the space to spend time with employees is critical to the success and growth of any company. He believes that every employee can contribute, stating that, 'They may not be CEO, they may not have a university degree but they are not stupid and they want to contribute and be heard'.

In his most recent role, Stephen's commitment to spend time with his employees was tested during significant upheaval in the organisation. Job losses were imminent—including his own. It is during these difficult times, when people are rightly frustrated and sometimes even angry, that 'the easiest thing to do is retreat to the man-cave or the ivory tower,' Stephen reflected. He knew, however, that it was during these times that he needed to be more present for employees.

Stephen suggested that 'connecting and engaging with people is not rocket science but it does require effort. If you don't personally think it's important then you won't do it'.

Prioritising can take a crisis

Sometimes it takes a crisis to realise that you have lost touch with what is going on for your people—that you no longer know what is real for them.

In 2015, ABC's *Four Corners* program reported on their investigation that had revealed a widespread practice of franchisees overworking and underpaying their workers, including 7-Eleven, Caltex, Domino's and Pizza Hut franchise owners. The investigation uncovered underpayments, predominantly to foreign students in the franchise sector.

Michael Smith was deputy chairman of 7-Eleven and had been on the board since 1999. Shortly after the underpayment scandal, Smith was appointed chairman of the company and was interviewed by *Boss* magazine. Smith explained why, as someone who had been with the business for many years, he took on the role of chairman: 'I was obviously part of the group who didn't see the problem...I have a deep sense of responsibility to fix this'.

Smith realised that by focusing on the retail customer, the 7-Eleven leadership group had lost touch with the grassroots of the business, the franchisees. Smith told *Boss* magazine the leadership group should have been closer to these businesses, 'including understanding the predominate cultures in our networks, and running our own stores'.

It was a classic case of not knowing what was real for their people. The board had focused on knowing what was real for their customers but had not understood what was happening in the world of their franchisees.

Smith then led the way to understand their franchisees better. He would often pop into 7-Eleven stores unannounced to talk with the franchisees, and he encouraged his other board members, CEO and senior leadership team to do the same. Official visits were also organised for the board members, who would all jump in a minibus and visit stores. But Smith also made a practice of dropping in at unexpected times — visiting stores at 1 am, for example. He said that he 'learnt more out of that than ten visits in the official mini-bus with the board'.

He also decided to spend time with franchisees and their families, including visiting the houses of franchisees to gain a greater understanding of their culture and challenges.

Smith even travelled to China, India and Pakistan to visit the extended families of franchisees. This was a deliberate strategy to firstly understand at a deeper level the cultural differences but also create a greater connection with their franchisees. A one-man videographer travelled with Smith and his wife to capture these stories, and the subsequent short videos will be shared internally.

Smith lives by the motto 'First seek to understand before you are understood'. When it comes to knowing what is real for your employees, this is good advice we could all learn from.

You need to find ways to understand your employees better, and to create an environment where they feel safe to provide feedback, offer opinions and talk about what is important for them.

Be a role model

Leaders need to be role models when it comes to providing feedback, challenging opinions and speaking truth to power. It seems a bit hypocritical if a leader tells their people to speak up when they are not seen doing that themselves.

You have no doubt read, heard and experienced firsthand the importance of role modelling from leaders, but it becomes essential if you want to create a culture of openness and people feeling free to speak their mind without retribution.

Simon Sinek has provided a great quote on this: 'Leaders are the ones who have the courage to go first and open a path for others to follow'. As a leader have the courage to role model this behaviour.

Get REAL now

- Understand the strong human instincts of self-preservation when asking for feedback.

- Create a safe environment where feedback can be shared.

- Ask probing questions and be prepared to sit in silence.

- Become a good, non-judgemental listener.

- Spend real time with your employees and, if necessary, schedule it in your diary, especially in times of change and uncertainty.

CONCLUSION

If you take just one thing away from this book, it should be to start communicating in a way that is more real and to lead in a way that is more authentic. Okay, maybe that's two things, but they are really not that hard.

However, I know from experience and from hearing the stories of those mentioned in this book that at times real communication and authentic leadership are easier said than done.

One of the hardest decisions I made with this book was to put an image of me on the front cover. I have never done that before, but I felt that I could not publish something about being real and authentic without this. Otherwise, I would just be a hypocrite!

Putting yourself out there can be daunting. Sharing personal stories can seem indulgent. Admitting your stuff-ups can be challenging. Taking a stand on what you believe in can feel scary. Not hiding behind acronyms and jargon and instead using real words can be conflicting. Asking for feedback and being prepared to listen to the truth can be confronting.

Yet having the courage to do this can mean we are seen as more approachable, more human, more engaging and more inspiring.

So I hope that what I have shown you will encourage you to do the same. We need real communication more than ever before, and now you know it can be done — it just needs you to embrace authentic leadership and to make a difference in your own world.

The people you lead and the customers you serve deserve nothing less.

It truly is time to get real. To just be you and lead true.

ARE YOU READY TO GET REAL?

Thank you for taking the time to read this book.

If you have enjoyed it and think I could help you and/or your company get real with communication and leadership, I would love the opportunity to add value.

If you want me to speak at your next conference, I promise to deliver an entertaining and educational talk on authentic leadership, real communication or business storytelling, or any combination of these.

If you want to train your employees on effectively using stories in business, I have been doing this for almost as long as PowerPoint has been around! (Well, not quite, but since 2004 — when storytelling in business wasn't even a thing.)

If you want your leaders to be better presenters and more engaging communicators, I can perform miracles in this area. Seriously, I can take beige to brilliant.

If you want yourself or your company to stand out as the experts, I can help. I teach clever professional people to raise their profile and influence in their industry to increase opportunities via Thought Leadership training.

If you want to communicate your company's values, purpose or strategy in a more engaging way, I can do that through training your leaders to use personal stories. (Don't call me if you want to communicate your company values by printing them on coffee mugs or posters.)

I also have some online programs available, including *Storytelling for Job Interviews* and *Business Storytelling*. You can check out what is on offer at my website (gabrielledolan.com/resources/programs and workshops).

I occasionally run public workshops but, if you have a team, training is like a good wine … always better when shared with others. So, talk to me about a tailored in-house training program.

Ways to get in touch:

- *gabrielledolan.com:* Subscribe to my newsletter and receive your 7-day Storytelling Starter Kit, along with other resources.

- *Jargonfreefridays.com:* Watch the videos, have a laugh and join the challenge.

- *Email:* enquiry@gabrielledolan.com

- *Phone:* +61 3 8383 2128

Or follow me on:

- *LinkedIn:* gabrielledolan

- *Facebook:* gabrielledolanconsulting

- *Instagram:* gabrielledolan.1

- *Twitter:* GabrielleDolan1

Ral

INDEX

GRATITUDE

My dear old Nana would always say, 'If you don't blow your own trumpet, then nobody else will'. I have taken her advice on many occasions but it is with enormous gratitude I now have other people being prepared to blow my trumpet for me. Here is what a few of them have to say about the work I have done with them.

Storytelling for business

Sometimes I wonder if Gabrielle Dolan has got an invisible magic wand because she seems to be able to mesmerise the audience so effortlessly. I was fortunate to have attended a few of her leadership workshops and, most recently, a Business Storytelling session that she delivered to nearly a thousand leaders in a financial institution. On reflection, I think she has mastered the art of 'teaching' people a skill/ capability in such an engaging manner because she really knows her stuff. More importantly, she is passionate about sharing with more people so that the business world is a better place if we get to practise what we've learnt from her. Her methods are always 'simple' and hence are more likely to be used after workshops or sessions—that's value for money!

Linda Yap, Head of Customer Optimisation, National Australia Bank

Gabrielle's storytelling workshop is very influential. Through excellent facilitation skills and lots of experience she helps all participants develop storytelling skills that are relevant, make an impact and add a personal touch to any context they are used in.

Sally Al-Nakshabandi, Head International Committee Red Cross, Humanitarian Leadership and Management School, Switzerland

❝ I recently attended Gabrielle's Business Storytelling Workshop in Melbourne and loved every minute of it! From the moment the workshop started it was clear it was going to be a fun learning environment. Gabrielle delivers the content in such an engaging way that you actually don't realise you're learning until you put the theory into practice. I highly recommend this workshop or working with Gabrielle to improve storytelling capability within your business.

Suzanne Richards, Internal Communications Manager, 7-Eleven, Australia

❝ I could not recommend Gabrielle more highly: this is a tough subject topic — senior leaders can be very suspicious of the benefit of storytelling — but Gabrielle drives home the message elegantly. She has a great connection with the audience whether they be CEOs of businesses or front line team leaders. Our 700 delegates had choices as to whether they attended Gabrielle's session or other sessions by other speakers: Gabrielle became the 'must see' of the event, with most of her sessions having 'standing room' only (and we gave her a big room to start with!!).

Not surprisingly she received the highest rating from all 700 delegates — the star of the event.

Joe McCollum, Group Human Resources Director at Spark, New Zealand

❝ Gabrielle's storytelling masterclass is one of those experiences you will never forget and you come out of it really bringing home something you can treasure for life. I can't recommend it highly enough for anyone who wants to be a better leader or just a better person!

Lucy Zheng, Managing Partner Business Bank, National Australia Bank

❝ Three weeks ago, I had the pleasure of being in one of Gabrielle's one-day storytelling workshops. It's always tough to take a day out of a busy week, but Gabrielle quickly gained the group's trust and had us engaged in sharing our superpowers, personal and professional stories.

I'm sharing this with you because Gabrielle made such a tremendous impact on the team — not only equipping us with relevant skills we could put straight into practice the next day, but also strengthening the team dynamics and bond. Gabrielle is truly the master of storytelling for business.

Michelle Hardie, Enterprise Business Development Manager, Amazon Web Services

Conference speaking

One of the best leadership speakers in the country. Authentic and real, which is perfect as that's her area of expertise. Your audiences will love Ral's presentations. World-class speaker.

Matt Church, Author, Speaker and Founder of Thought Leaders

Gabrielle Dolan is an inspirational speaker who draws from her experience as a global thought leader on authentic leadership and business storytelling to connect with and wow audiences across the globe. We had the great fortune to engage Gabrielle as the opening keynote speaker for our 2017 IABC World Conference in Washington, D.C. In front of our international group of more than 1000 people, she demonstrated an exceptional ability to capture and challenge our audience while delivering some great tips about becoming better leaders and communicators using the art of storytelling. It was one of the highest rated general sessions for our World Conference. I highly recommend Gabrielle as a keynote speaker for your next event.

Sarah McLaughlin Porteous, Director of Communications at City of New Orleans, USA

Her presentation was very effective in drawing attention to what organisations are doing 'wrong' and how to be better. Her generous approach gave practical solutions and inspirational guidance to help our organisations be more authentic—all with an engaging style of delivery that at times had us rolling with laughter.

Neil Griffiths, Senior Manager, Global Communications at ERM, United Kingdom

Engaging speaker—funny, thought-provoking—and use of real-life stories is very impactful and easy to apply. Thanks Gabrielle!

Carly (Nider) Khanna, Vice President at AE Works, USA

" Gabrielle (AKA Ral) is a genius in all things leadership and storytelling. Underneath this genius is a commitment to living (and teaching others) to live with authenticity. What you see with Ral is what you get. Which interestingly makes her one of the best leadership speakers in the country—she's completely herself on stage...which is surprisingly rare and part of what makes her a world-class speaker. Her work is transformational. Ral has a deep integrity and wisdom. She has fun while making a profound difference. If you get a chance to work with her, grab it. She rocks.

Peter Cook, CEO of Thought Leaders Business School, Australia

" Gabrielle, it takes a certain kind of skill to keep 850 people engaged for two hours, and you did it with ease. Thank you for joining us, sharing your knowledge, and being easy to work with.

Kirsty Freeman, HR Consultant,
National Australia Bank

Thought leadership

" Since attending the Thought Leadership Intensive my creativity is on overdrive. I have a much better framework for how to organise my thinking. I'm reading more strategically, writing more and speaking in public more effectively. She's a genius!

Denise Collazo, Chief of Staff,
Faith in Action, USA

" Gabrielle's Thought Leadership Intensive two-day course is not only inspiring and motivating but also a practical way to organise myself as a new consultant and independent thought leader developing my own models and IP. I really recommend this experience. Gabrielle is also highly engaging and builds your confidence effortlessly.

Paul Matthews, Founder and Director,
The Comms Coach, Australia

" Gabrielle is always inspiring, and what is great about this program is that it is set up so that it becomes ingrained in your professional life.

Can highly recommend to anyone looking to find a way to channel their voice with impact.

Claudette Leeming, Head of Property Strategy and Perfomance, Australia Post

Gabrielle's Thought Leadership workshop is life changing! Anyone seeking to increase their profile, influence and business or career opportunities should seriously think about enrolling in this program!

Elizabeth Foley, speaker and writer on financial literacy, Australia

A privilege to be part of Gabrielle's Thought Leadership Program. The two days provided a catalyst to step out of my comfort zone and be 'heard' as a thought leader. Great framework, tools and ongoing 'nudges' from Gabrielle to stay on track.

Jennifer Darbyshire, General Counsel, Governance, National Australia Bank

I had the greatest pleasure of partaking in Gabrielle's Thought Leadership Intensive course—I was blown away by her delivery, passion and content. I came away exhausted and completely inspired. Highly recommended!

Susie Greig Rouffignac, Philanthropy Manager, The Women's Foundation at The Royal Women's Hospital, Australia

Also available from Gabrielle Dolan ...

'*Stories for Work* will give you everything you need to be more inspiring
and effective in your business communications. A must read business book!'
—Michael Ebeid, CEO & Managing Director, SBS

stories
for
work
the essential
guide to business
storytelling

Gabrielle Dolan

WILEY

Available in print, audio and e-book formats